ZEYNEP FADILLIOĞLU

LUXURY REDEFINED

ZEYNEP FADILLIOĞLU
LUXURY REDEFINED

Catherine Shaw

RIZZOLI
NEW YORK

New York · Paris · London · Milan

For my beloved daughter Selin.

Table of Contents

Foreword

THE HON. SIR MICHAEL KADOORIE

I am honoured to have been asked to provide a few introductory remarks to this magnificent testament to the achievements of Zeynep Fadıllıoğlu. It also seems particularly appropriate timing, as this publication is being issued shortly after the opening of our Peninsula Hotel in Istanbul, to which Zeynep has made such a significant contribution.

The Istanbul hotel's development has involved some five years of constant close collaboration, a journey together with our partners, Galataport Holdings, that has been exceptionally fruitful as well as a great pleasure.

Our hotel company is renowned for its very long-term perspective, and when we consider any new hotel project, it is only after a lengthy and painstaking evaluation process. This approach is the same for the development stage. The highest technical and professional standards are required, and in this respect Zeynep's creativity, principles, and values are highlighted by her profound interest in, and respect for, heritage and tradition—values truly aligned with our own.

The location at Galataport provided us with a unique opportunity to restore one of the most significant waterfront sites on the Bosphorus, coming with the responsibility to restore its heritage properties with due sensitivity. Zeynep grew up on the Bosphorus and Istanbul is her city, thus she was able to provide her deep insight into this particular aspect, while also incorporating more contemporary elements thanks to her extensive international experience. Throughout the process, she demonstrated a profound understanding of both the city's heritage and the Peninsula's specific ethos, thereby creating a marriage of tradition with contemporary, elegant, and sophisticated luxury.

The Peninsula Istanbul is thus a showcase of Zeynep's design talent, and, of course, I welcome you most warmly to visit the hotel to experience the unique environment that, together with our partners, we have created in one of the world's great cities. In the hotel, you will see how effectively Zeynep has managed to layer different design elements—such as colour, palette, and texture—to create a refined yet glamorous atmosphere. Her attention to design detail is unrivalled, as is evident throughout the hotel. This is exemplified in such features as the intricate mother-of-pearl inlays in furniture, a tribute to Ottoman traditional patterns reinterpreted with subtle nuances; the *kilim* motif in carpets; and inlay details in bedroom walls and bathroom floors.

It was also most pleasing to see the attention she devoted to the back-of-house areas of the hotel, such as the staff dining area, which has the feel of a luxury restaurant. These are, of course, not areas seen by guests, but they are hugely important in the provision of a quality environment for our highly valued staff.

I should emphasize what a great pleasure it has been for both our project team and myself to have worked with Zeynep so closely on The Peninsula Istanbul. Creating such a hotel is a challenging and complex process, one that can be potentially fraught with difficulty. To manage this successfully requires commitment, professionalism, and patience, and in this regard Zeynep's dedication and passion have been inspiring to us all.

Zeynep Fadıllıoğlu deserves our most sincere thanks for her contribution to The Peninsula Istanbul in particular, and I pay tribute to her wider achievements as portrayed in this impressive publication.

The Hon. Sir Michael Kadoorie
Chairman
The Hongkong and Shanghai Hotels, Limited

Introduction

CATHERINE SHAW

I've lost count of the number of people who, hearing that I was to visit Istanbul for the first time, insisted that I must meet the Turkish interior designer Zeynep Fadıllıoğlu.

Hers is an unusual story, largely one of innovation: the first woman to design a mosque—an audaciously modern mosque at that—as well as the interiors of many chic and popular restaurants, clubs, and bars; a host of groundbreaking interior projects across Europe, Türkiye, and the Middle East; and in 2023, a glamorous new hotel on the edge of the Bosphorus, The Peninsula Istanbul.

There are multiple compelling stories to relate about this remarkable designer, and the thread that runs through them is Zeynep's thoughtful approach to design and her intuitive ability to create spaces that communicate both warmth and character. As Britain's eminent master craftsman the then Viscount Linley remarks, "Zeynep is a designer of supremely elegant interiors. She combines her national heritage with modern practicality. Her ingenious layering of textures and colors gives her spaces a timeless feel. She successfully contrasts traditional craft with contemporary comfort."

In some ways Zeynep is a reflection of Istanbul, the city where she was born, where East and West converge and dissolve into each other—a city that for centuries has been a confluence of culture and creativity, and the integration of history and novelty. Her childhood home was a lavish Italian-style palazzo on the European shore of the Bosphorus, and her earliest memories are of living among a cabinet-of-curiosities-style collection of antiques. It was a culturally rich environment, peopled by memorable figures: among others the aristocratic Hungarian governess who taught Zeynep and her siblings to speak other languages and to waltz, as well as legendary Russian ballet dancer Rudolf Nureyev (1938–1993), who visited them when he performed *Sleeping Beauty* at the Istanbul State Opera and Ballet in 1986. It was a fortunate, extraordinary upbringing.

As a student, Zeynep excelled at sports and mathematics. She was a national downhill ski champion, and initially intended to pursue a career in computer programming. Serendipitously, a Damascene conversion came as her father's encouragement to "try something creative" coincided with her own wish to spend more time in London, where she began to study Art History and Design. He redirected her mathematical attention toward a newfound career, driven in large part by a fascination with the traditions of the ancient Byzantine, Anatolian, Seljuk, and Ottoman arts and crafts. "I felt an instant affinity," Zeynep recalls. "Suddenly everything just made sense."

Not long after Zeynep married in 1980, her husband, Metin, who owned a group of restaurants, bars, and clubs both in Istanbul and abroad, suggested they might work together to set the mood in his establishments. The result has been a resounding success: Zeynep treats each new project as a unique journey, working closely with artists and artisans to create custom décor pieces and site-specific installations, introducing interiors full of texture, pattern, and color that are also rooted in practicality. She arranges unusual finds, some precious and others simply interesting, in intriguing vignettes, creating an atmosphere that diners find instinctively appealing.

Since establishing her eponymous studio—more of a creative, collaborative atelier than design firm—in Istanbul in 1995, Zeynep has worked all over the world, building up an award-winning portfolio that stands out for its diversity as well as its richly layered, distinctive use of colors and materials. She is also renowned for designing more than fifteen mosques. Still, the designer is unfailingly modest about her role. She surrounds herself with multidisciplinary creatives who each contribute their specialties to a project—from art, architecture, and crafts to product design—Zeynep is always open to different opinions and indeed seeks these out for she values the eclecticism and expertise that is all around her. "Design is less about 'a moment of genius' from an individual creator. I think that creativity is always more powerful when you share a common purpose," she explains. Her Istanbul office, a classic five-story house with a lush garden on the Bosphorus, was once a comfortable home. Stuffed with antiques, art, and design, it retains a familial, informal, and unrestrained atmosphere while operating as a laboratory for ideas.

There is an inherent cross-pollination in Zeynep's creative process. Not only does she work on an exciting variety of projects, but she finds stimulus in a wide range of sources—from nature and landscape to architecture, fashion, design, art, and photography. She is constantly traveling, seeking inspiration for the the finest texture and details in her work. Zeynep also often dives into her own archive, choosing colors and patterns from her magnificent collections of vintage textiles and antique ceramics to translate into dense embroideries, artisan weaves, and three-dimensional forms. These deliver up conceptual objects in which artistic values and functionality come together. In some ways, Zeynep's eye is therefore as much that of an archaeologist as a designer, since she always unearths interesting things that create a connection between the setting and its owner—there is always such a sense of discovery when you visit one of her projects.

Zeynep custom designs many of her furnishings and finishes, thus ensuring every detail speaks to the space rather than the other way around. Her choice of materials is refined—bronze and wood, ceramic and rock crystal—and her forms are diverse. It is design with an artisanal soul, with an ageless feel that can be handed down to future generations, and reflects how Zeynep thinks beyond individual pieces of furniture and accessories to look at how people's lives are changing.

She is not interested in stylistic gesture. Her practice is stimulated by modernization, mixing the old with the new, and drawing on contrasting cultural references, boldly linking different influences from Ottoman hammams (bathhouses) to Japanese anime and Chinese feng shui. Zeynep's focus is to move beyond what many have come to expect from Turkish designers, and to deliver what is socially and culturally relevant today, and also has global appeal.

Even as Zeynep's style evolves, her designs continue to tell stories. Her sensitive grasp of the spirit of a project helps produce a strong concept as she explores and analyzes the needs of the user, selecting materials, processes, and finishes to convey a mood. Each space, each project therefore, has its own lively and inspired narrative, not only exhilarating in appearance, but also thoughtfully conceived and developed in a clear sequence so that every space has a framework and a dénouement. Her interest is in atmosphere, and the relationship between the tangible and the intangible: "Space is not static."

As we collaborated on this book, I visited many of the places Zeynep has designed, and I have come to see firsthand that her approach is always a response to specific conditions and objectives. Zeynep naturally and automatically combines design rigor with intuitive originality, elevating materials and objects to form a new vocabulary that imbues each project with its own distinctive personality, tone, and emotion. She keeps the avant-garde and tradition in constant dialogue, but concentrates on fostering a feeling before defining a style. Thus, her interiors across the globe always possess a strong sense of integrity and place, intelligent use of spatial planning, and a keen eye for composition and detailing.

With such an elaborate story to tell, it feels natural that this book should step away from the traditional chronological detailing of projects that make up the designer's prolific, productive, decades-long career. Instead Zeynep, in her typically open and generous fashion, has chosen to describe the influences and thinking behind her work that allow her to excel and endure. The result is an informal conversation in her own words about how a natural curiosity about art, a passion for craftsmanship, and a profound interest in cultural heritage guide her design ethos, are integral to her design narrative, and underlie her steadfast commitment to beauty and originality.

Page 6: Wardrobes made of high-gloss cedar wood, especially chosen for its scent, 2017. Private residence.

Previous page: Zeynep Fadıllıoğlu at The Peninsula Istanbul, Türkiye, 2023.

Next page: The lobby of The Peninsula Istanbul, Türkiye (2023) is located in a restored historic 20th-century landmark ferry terminal in Karaköy, Istanbul, as photographed by renowned artist, Ahmet Ertuğ.

Nature

" To live!
Like a tree alone and free.
Like a forest in brotherhood.
This yearning is ours. **"**

NÂZIM HIKMET,[1] *THE EPIC OF THE LIBERATION WAR*[2]

Opposite: Glass facade. Şakirin
Mosque, Istanbul, Türkiye, 2009.

1. (1902–1963) Modern Turkish poet
   and playwright.

2. *Kuvayi Milliye*, (Istanbul: Adam
   Yayıncılık, 1987), p. 90.

Previous page, left: Şakirin Mosque, Istanbul, Türkiye, 2009. William Pye, *Untitled*, 2009, water sculpture symbolizing a reflection of the universe.

Previous page, right: Şakirin Mosque, Istanbul, Türkiye, 2009. The dome is clad with aluminum composite panels, a modern interpretation of the traditional form.

Opposite: Şakirin Mosque, Istanbul, Türkiye, 2009. The prayer hall.

Next page: Şakirin Mosque, Istanbul, Türkiye, 2009. *Minbar* decoration: carnation petals inlaid in resin; circular shapes represent the universe.

Page 26: Şakirin Mosque, Istanbul, Türkiye, 2009. The *minbar*.

Page 27: Şakirin Mosque, Istanbul, Türkiye, 2009. Glass pendeloques inspired by light shining through raindrops.

I always start each design by thinking about the needs and expectations of whoever will use the spaces—and then I explore the surrounding landscape.

The Şakirin Mosque in Üsküdar, Istanbul (2009) is a good example of how I approach projects that may be particularly complex. The mosque, built by the Şakir family in memory of İbrahim and Semiha Şakir, is located at the entrance of the Karacaahmet Cemetery, one of Istanbul's oldest graveyards, which has some particularly beautiful sycamore, laurel, and hackberry trees. Some are over 2,000 years old so, right from the start, I knew that it was essential that, while I needed to design an inspiring, efficient, and comfortable building for people who would pray there, the architecture should complement its setting in a deferential, nuanced way. It was considered very unusual for a woman to design a mosque, so before I began I also consulted very closely with theologians, historians, and worshipers.

The building is strikingly modern and it integrates views through a facade that comprises two layers: an inner structural glass layer featuring a decorative pattern that evokes Al Surah al-Nur, a well known verse in the Qur'an that is a parable about the light of Allah, and an exterior slanted layer of metal mesh in six decorative patterns. The sunlight streaming through the enormous windows bathes the imam and worshipers in its reflection, and provides a panoramic yet fleeting glimpse of the surrounding trees.

Creating a sense of place is not just about views. I also express nature and landscape through building materials and finishes, art and textiles, to create a multisensory experience. At the Şakirin Mosque, I designed a contemporary asymmetrical low-lying chandelier with teardrop-inspired glass pendeloques to represent the spirit of nature. The resin surface of the *minbar* is inlaid with carnations that symbolize devotion and add a sense of depth and richness to the interior in an understated, gracious way. The mosque's prominent single-domed ceiling is hand painted in the earthy terra-cotta tones of Tophane-style pottery, creating an ombré effect, while outside, in the courtyard, smaller domes above the arcaded courtyard perimeter are painted with floral patterns.

Previous page: Sixteenth-century map showing historical Istanbul's Galata and Karaköy districts, and the location of The Peninsula Istanbul, Türkiye. Matrakçı Nasuh, *Beyan-ı Menazil-i Sefer-i Irakeyn-i Sultan Süleyman Han* (Suleiman the Magnificent's Iraq Campaign), 1533–1536.

Left: Richard Hudson, *Tear*, 2021, polished mirrored steel. The Peninsula Istanbul, Türkiye, 2023.

Above: The Peninsula Istanbul, Türkiye, 2023. Early site-section sketch by Enea Landscape Architecture.

The Peninsula Istanbul (2023), a luxury hotel located on the very edge of the Bosphorus, was a project that called for a very different approach to that of the Şakirin Mosque. It has a fascinating urban setting near to the Galata Bridge in Karaköy, which is an important commercial center and one of the oldest and most historic districts of the city. I wanted to create a sense of escape to a calm and restful sanctuary, so I combined a sensuous interior color palette of soft and more intense blues, as well as the shimmering golden hues of sunsets, with rich textures and patterns to create a subliminal connection with nature. The lobby has an earthy clay-colored carpet and, in the spa, the thermal treatment room is completely swathed in darker, cooler shades of blue, while the relaxation room has a beautiful cerulean mosaic pattern that takes delicate cues from the subdued beauty of the Bosphorus in winter.

For designers, it is always very important to understand the wider context beyond the project site. When Enzo Enea, The Peninsula Istanbul's landscape architect, first joined the team, we sailed up and down both sides of the Bosphorus to see how closely nature and the architecture of *yalıs*, the city's traditional waterside summer residences, are intertwined. At the hotel, Enzo envisioned a lush green park with secret niches to discover. The park harmoniously links the different buildings and modes of use, including the guest room balconies and the buildings' vast rooftops. A magnificent terrace is planted with pomegranate trees, which are especially striking when viewed from the water.

Left: The Peninsula Istanbul, Türkiye, 2023. View from the Bosphorus.

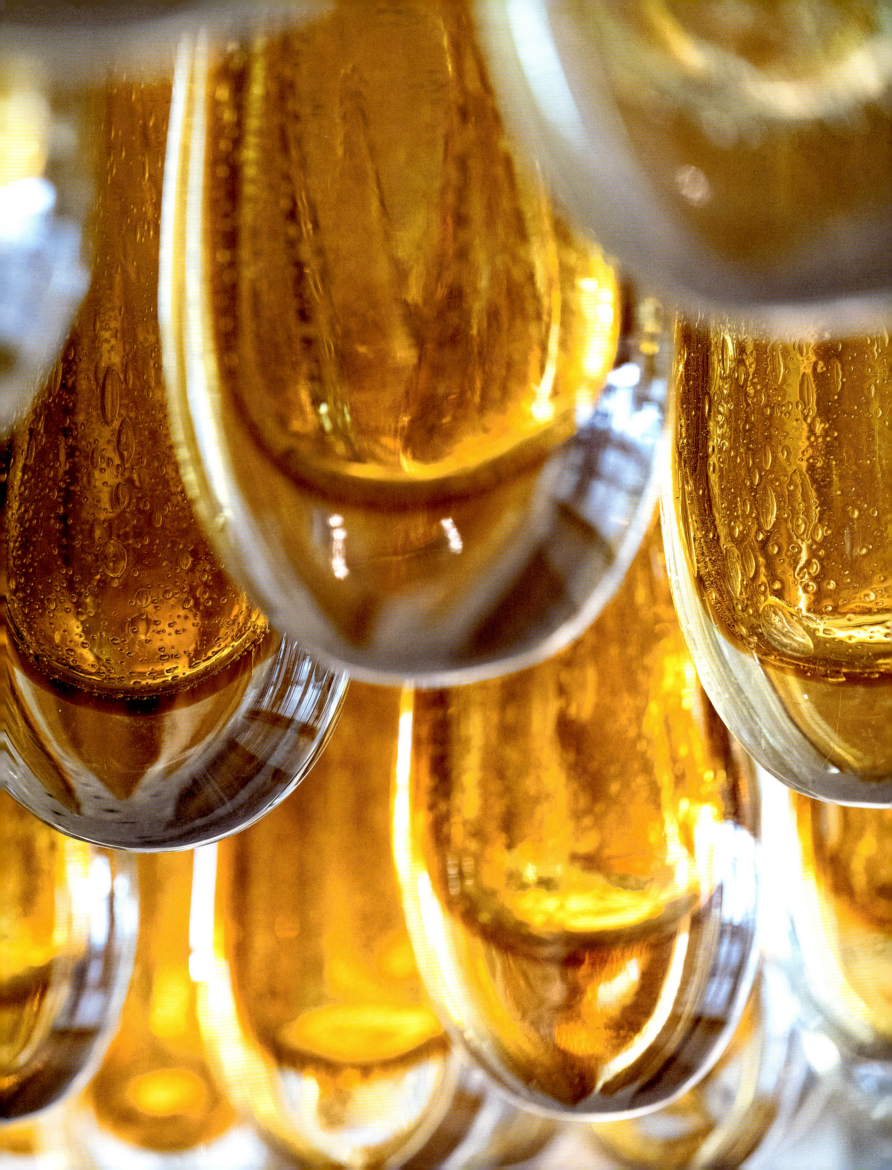

I have a deep love and respect for nature, and it has always been one of the most important inspirational elements in my work. Nature makes everything feel softer. I like to think of it as something that caresses one's eye. I take inspiration from many different landscapes and often visit gardens when I travel. I am fascinated by how landscapes are so dramatically different around the world. The moss garden of Kokedera, in western Kyoto, Japan, is one of the most memorable for me, expressing Zen Buddhist culture through its calm and reflective landscaping and exquisite temple.

Although my Istanbul home is quite far from the center of the city, I actually chose it because I loved the eclectic collection of trees in the garden. Some are over 100 years old, and together they created such a powerful, lush context that we bought the property, even though the house itself was quite dilapidated and needed major restoration work.

Previous page, left: The Peninsula Istanbul, Türkiye, 2023. Glass droplets hand-blown by Lasvit for a ballroom chandelier.

Previous page, right: The Peninsula Istanbul, Türkiye, 2023. Ceramic tiles made by Gorbon in different tones of turquoise. Sicis glass mosaic in turquoise, gold, and beige.

Above: Zeynep's home, Istanbul, Türkiye. Berna Bal, 2023, digital illustration.

Right: Private mansion, Tarabya, Istanbul, Türkiye, 2015. Vintage lighthouse mirror.

Left: Beach tents, Cultural Village, Katara, Doha, Qatar, 2015. An aluminum-and-glass structure provides lightness and transparency while the drapery creates privacy.

Next page, left: Kuum 29 Beach Club Restaurant, Bodrum, Türkiye, 2011. Beach club designed to create a private bay.

Next page, right: Matrakçı Nasuh, *Ottoman Tents*, from *Beyan-ı Menazil-i Sefer-i Irakeyn-i Sultan Süleyman Han* (Suleiman the Magnificent's Iraq Campaign), 1533–1536.

Emirgan Park along the Bosphorus in Sarıyer is also a particular inspiration for me. It is very large—around 470,000 square meters—and contains rare Turkish and Aleppo pines, as well as Japanese, Lebanon, and Himalayan cedars. The tulip gardens are spectacular. Although most people associate tulips with Holland, they originally grew wild on the Central Asian steppes and their cultivation began in the Ottoman Empire, so the park has revived our traditional appreciation of these striking, vibrant flowers. I always look forward to spring, when the blossoms of the Judas trees cover the shores of the Bosphorus with brilliant swathes of rich pinkish-purple. These floral influences appear in many of my design projects, from colorful tiles to textiles with patterns that evoke their natural form and beauty.

I've always liked to play with the sense of being neither completely indoors, nor outdoors—adding a touch of fantasy to the experience of being immersed in nature. People in Istanbul love to be outside, and restaurant seating on pavements and terraces is always the most popular. Where homes have gardens, there are often small, detached pavilions and gazebos that allow for the natural setting to be enjoyed in comfort. Such buildings are an integral part of our Ottoman architectural heritage; the English word kiosk actually comes from the Turkish *köşk*, generally referring to a small garden pavilion. You can see these along the edge of the Bosphorus, where many of the homes have simple yet elegant outdoor structures for people to eat meals in and relax. They can be found in Emirgan Park too, where they were constructed by the Ottoman governor of Egypt and Sudan during the nineteenth century. Restored in the 1970s, the Sarı Köşk (Yellow Pavilion) features traditional Ottoman architecture, the Beyaz Köşk (White Pavilion) was constructed in a neoclassical style, and the Pembe Köşk (Pink Pavilion) has become a popular wedding venue.

My own design portfolio of outdoor shelters is very diverse and includes everything from simple pergolas to intricate pavilions and grand Ottoman tents. They are not always traditional in style: sometimes I take cues from a historical architectural form and express it in a minimalist, but still elegant, way with modern materials, such as metals or concrete. Whether it looks traditional or modern, the design always reflects and extends the architecture of the building and its surroundings. Even though I've designed such structures for dramatically different locations—from Bodrum to St.Tropez, Baku to London—and each design calls for a different permutation, they are all about being closer to nature.

Courtyards have also always been an important part of Turkish culture, and can be seen as neither completely indoors nor out. In 2022, I worked closely with the luxury interiors company de Gournay to create an intricate, contemporary, hand-painted metallic-silk and silver-leaf wallpaper, featuring an Ottoman courtyard with an exuberant array of peacocks, trees, flowers, and pavilions that bring a very delicate, captivating, and nostalgic hint of nature to an interior.

Blurring the perceived boundaries between indoors and out sometimes means transporting elements from one context to another to cast light on them from a different perspective. Some people were quite shocked when I first carried indoor furniture, carpets, and cushions outside onto lawns in order to create enticing al fresco spaces for events. Carpets were normally either used for religious purposes or were laid inside; however, I have always enjoyed the unexpected juxtaposition of indoor furnishings with balconies, terraces, and gardens, and the unique atmosphere this creates.

My husband, Metin, was in the restaurant business for many years, and at one point owned and managed thirty-six restaurants, clubs, and bars in Istanbul, Paris, Monaco, and London. I designed many of these spaces with nature in mind. Vaniköy 29 in Istanbul (1985), the first outdoor club on the Asian side of the Bosphorus, became especially famous because guests arriving by boat would literally have crossed over from Europe in just five minutes—and could then eat and dance right on the water's edge. The concept, from the pool and sundeck to floor cushions for lounging under tented canopies, was rather revolutionary because it was dazzling yet outdoors, and therefore immersed in nature.

In 2007, I was commissioned by a client to create a Greek-inspired setting for a special one-night dining event on a small, privately owned Mediterranean island (Event-South, Göcek Bay in Muğla). I built the nomadic theme around textiles, inspired by the paintings of Italian realist artist Fausto Zonaro (1854–1929) that featured sultans' tents on sailboats in Ottoman times. Tents were a prized form of architecture for the Ottomans, seen as lavish mobile palaces. Some had several levels, and were decorated with intricate embroidery. I took inspiration from these and added a cyan color palette to evoke Greece.

Textiles are a wonderful way to bring the outside in. My paternal great-grandfather, Salih Bosna (1865–1940), established the first cotton factory in Türkiye under the Ottoman Empire. My maternal grandfather, Rifat Pekiş (1901–1951), started a modern silk-textile business during the 1930s, and was a great art patron and collector, so naturally we were surrounded by beautiful fabrics at home. I remember how my grandmother Hayriye Pekiş (b. 1909–1960) would wear clothes made from a variety of luxurious handwoven materials, like Venetian Fortuny and the richly patterned local Turkish textiles from Bursa in northwestern Türkiye.

Previous page: Design concept for a heritage hotel, Rome: speakeasy bar, inspired by nineteenth-century Istanbul. Chairs upholstered in modern *ikat*-patterned, brushed velvet capitoné stools, and Iznik-style wall tiles.

Opposite: Ulus 29 Restaurant Club, Istanbul, Türkiye, c. 2018. Natural upholstery fabrics, straw inset lampshade, and Japanese-inspired bamboo *sudare* blinds.

I love traveling to countries where fabric remains a fundamental part of daily life and wider cultural heritage. Over the years, I have been fortunate enough to assemble an extensive collection of textiles, including antique handwoven and embroidered pieces from countries such as India and Japan, and these provide daily visual inspiration. They are also a resource for creating unique design pieces. At the Masterpiece London art fair (2022), for example, I showed a pair of voluptuous signature Sedir Mini armchairs, upholstered in an eclectic combination of antique fabrics.

Natural elements are also expressed in my work through specific art choices: for example, I included a contemporary water sculpture by British artist William Pye (b. 1938) in my design for the courtyard of the Şakirin Mosque. The polished stainless-steel hemisphere has water emerging at its apex that runs down over its outer surface in waves, and this gives the space a sense of tranquility.

One of my favorite pieces of digital art is also water-inspired, and is by Turkish-American artist and filmmaker Kutluğ Ataman (b. 1961). It comprises three horizontal videos of the Bosphorus, filmed at various times of the day in different seasons. Each video is dramatically dissimilar in terms of its texture and color, yet they all reflect the same body of water. To me, this felt like bringing the Bosphorus indoors, so I decided to install it in a prominent position at the Ulus 29 Restaurant Club in Istanbul (1993), a restaurant that is perched on the side of a steep, undulating mountainside overlooking the strait. The compelling—almost hypnotic—videos emphasize the natural surroundings and provide a connection to the water that can be seen in the distance.

For me, designing interiors with a sensory appreciation and experience of nature is not only about aesthetics but, just as Nâzim Hikmet hints in the poem quoted at the start of this chapter, it is always also about nurturing a sense of salubrity, strength, and spiritual well-being.

Left: Ulus 29 Restaurant Club, Istanbul, Türkiye, c.1993. Tented structure by Alev Sağlam created from antique Italian, English, and Turkish textiles; handmade terra-cotta floor tiles; and a plexiglass domed roof.

The Princes' Islands Boutique Hotel
Club House, Istanbul, Türkiye, 2017.
Outdoor terrace (*above*) and view
toward the balcony (*right*).

Previous page: The Princes' Islands,
Istanbul, Türkiye, 2017. Interior
design by Zeynep Fadıllıoğlu Design
for a *köşk*-inspired clubhouse and
boutique hotel.

Left: Six Senses Kocataş Mansions,
Istanbul, Türkiye, 2019. Concept
design by Zeynep Fadıllıoğlu Design
for the interior of a restored
waterside boutique hotel.

Right: Kutluğ Ataman, *Su (Water)*, 2012, video artwork, private collection. Displayed at Ulus 29 Restaurant Club, Istanbul, Türkiye, c. 2012.

Above and opposite: Pool house, private mansion, Tarabya, Istanbul, Türkiye, 2015, where full-height windows and wood accents bring nature inside.

Next page: Ulus 29 Restaurant Club, Istanbul, Türkiye, c. 2014. Patinated ceiling with a *muqarnas* border, stained bamboo wall paneling, and agate bar.

Opposite: Ulus 29 Restaurant Club,
Istanbul, Türkiye, c. 2014. Indian
rock-crystal sconce, set against
nature-themed Hermès wallpaper.

For me, designing interiors with a sensory appreciation and experience of nature is not only about aesthetics but, just as Nâzim Hikmet hints in the poem quoted at the start of this chapter, it is always also about nurturing a sense of salubrity, strength, and spiritual well-being.

Art

" Art divorced from life has no great significance … To bridge this gap is very arduous, especially for those who are gifted and technically proficient; but it is only when the gap is bridged that our life becomes integrated and art an integral expression of ourselves. **"**

JIDDU KRISHNAMURTI[1]

Left: Peter Beard, *untitled mural*, 2018, color print collage, 6.5 m x 13 m. Nahita restaurant, Boston, United States, 2018.

1. Jiddu Krishnamurti, "Chapter 8: Art, Beauty and Creation, Education and the Significance of Life" (1953). Available via https://www.jkrishnamurti.org/content/chapter-8-art-beauty-and-creation

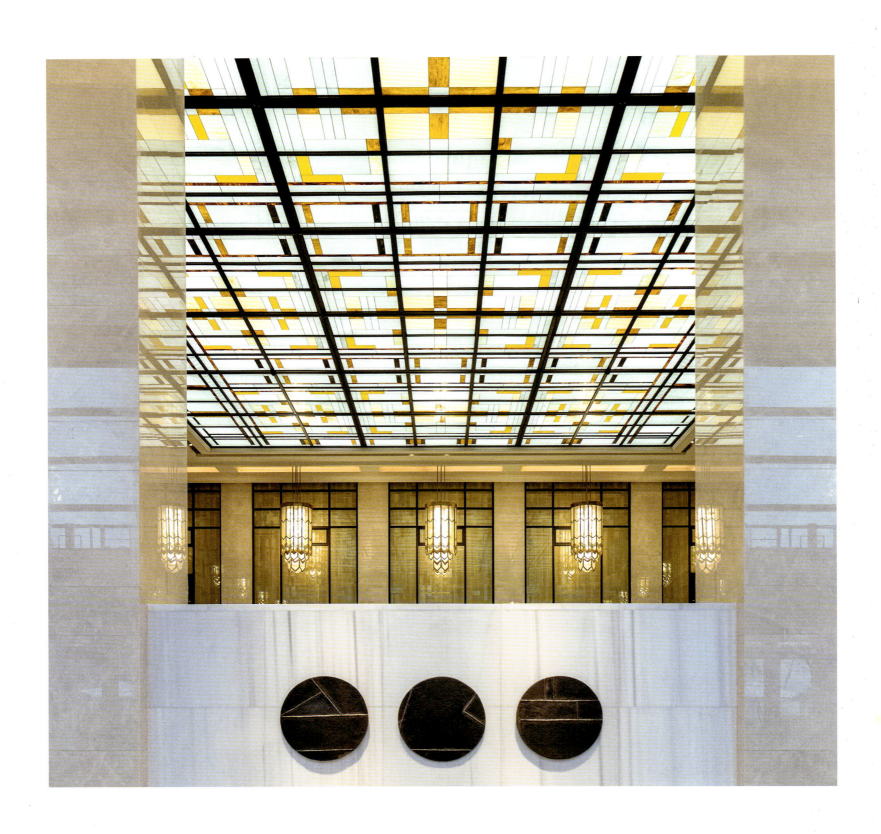

Above: Turhan Çetin, *Topographic Images*, c. 2008. Iron sculptures below a Bauhaus-inspired geometric glass ceiling. The Peninsula Istanbul, Türkiye, 2023.

Opposite: Zühtü Müridoğlu, *Unknown*, 1984, figurative bronze sculpture. Glimpsed between sliding doors painted to look like leather. Private residence, Istanbul, Türkiye, 2005.

Opposite: Nuri İyem, *Portrait of a Young Woman*, 1968, oil on canvas. Zeynep's home, Istanbul, Türkiye.

I was thirteen when Father took me to a charity auction in Istanbul and I bought my first work of art. I immediately fell in love with a portrait of a young woman painted by Turkish modern figurative artist Nuri İyem (1915–2005), and it still hangs in my home today. I grew up in a house with wonderful European art all around me, but this was the first time I had looked at something and decided myself whether to buy it or not. After that, each year my father and I would buy one more piece of art, so I gradually began to build up an appreciation of painting and sculpture.

For me, a room without art lacks a soul. It is such an important part of how we express ourselves. Art is therefore an integral part of each of my design projects, whether for public or private interiors. I buy a wide range of works of art both by well-known and emerging artists, and we also commission pieces for specific settings. We always take time to understand and reflect on our clients' tastes before developing mood boards. Although I don't paint or sculpt myself, I visualize my designs in a similar way, adding layers of colors and textures to create further dimensions. I was pleased, therefore, when the renowned artist Ömer Uluç (1931–2010) once remarked that he could see that I create spaces and places as if they were paintings.

I especially enjoy helping a client create their home. In 1997, in Hampstead, London, I worked closely with the owner to make it a luxurious yet livable space, bridging the classic and contemporary. It was to be centered around her substantial art collection, which included paintings and sculptures, so we focused on integrating the pieces in a natural, organic way, adding layers of visual interest and textures in each room through custom-designed furnishings and surfaces. To create a sense of discovery, for example, we added curtains of metal thread embroidered for us by the textile designer Alev Sağlam (b. 1964). Alev had recently graduated from studying fashion, and her embroidery was so artful that I knew it would be right for the curtains, which I felt deserved as much care and attention as a ball gown.

Above and opposite: Private
residence and collection,
Hampstead, London, UK, 1997.

Next page: Jaume Plensa, *Ines'
World I*, 2012, marble and concrete
(*left*), and Anselm Reyle, *Eternity*,
2008, bronze (*right*). Private *yalı*,
Istanbul, Türkiye, 2014.

Antony Gormley, *Human Body, Sublimate XXII*, 2008, bright welded mild steel blocks. Divans by Zeynep Fadıllıoğlu Design, chandelier by Mathieu Lustrerie, coffee tables by Hervé Van der Straeten, and chairs by Mark Brazier-Jones. Private *yalı*, Istanbul, Türkiye, 2014.

In 2014, I worked on a particularly beautiful *yalı* on the Bosphorus, where the owners had a wonderfully eclectic and expansive collection of art, ranging from traditional Far Eastern and European masterpieces and fine antiquities to avant-garde contemporary paintings, sculpture, and objects.

The house is arranged over four floors with a grand, sweeping staircase. Its traditional architecture and spacious high-ceilinged rooms provide plenty of wall space for hanging large works of art. My first task was to restore the house to its original beauty, stripping away previous renovations to reveal the intrinsic power of the structure and the red patina of its traditional Turkish walls to create a new backdrop.

My design concept focused on calling attention to the art collection. But a home is not a gallery, and in this case, since both the husband and wife had exceptional but very diverse tastes in art in terms of style, mediums, and eras, instead of creating a different look for each floor—which would have separated their lives—I looked for a fresh way to mix the classic and contemporary. I did this by juxtaposing different pieces: for example, an outstanding self-portrait by the acclaimed abstract artist Princess Fahrelnissa Zeid (1901–1991), who was known for her colorful kaleidoscopic motifs, with a large concave sculpture that acts as a mirror by contemporary British-Indian sculptor Sir Anish Kapoor CBE (b. 1954). We also added furnishings, including an intricate contemporary pendant lampshade, and a pair of striking geometric marble consoles by French designer Hervé Van der Straeten (b. 1965). I wanted the house to feel like a home for both of the owners, so it was wonderful to hear, after the couple had moved in, that they felt the design had brought them closer together.

The owners and I paid particular attention to the garden and the arrangement of three large sculptures near the waterside pavilion: an elegant, monumental white-marble and concrete piece by Spanish visual artist Jaume Plensa (b. 1955); an abstract bronze of undulating curves by German artist Anselm Reyle (b. 1970); and the figure of a man made by French interdisciplinary creator Xavier Veilhan (b. 1963) from folded sheets of stainless steel. I wanted to evoke a sense of conversation between the figures, the house and pavilion, and the Bosphorus.

Alex Katz, *Sarah Mearns*, 2011, oil on linen. Chandelier and cocktail table by Donghia. Side table, candlesticks, and table lamp by Hervé Van der Straeten. Private *yalı*, Istanbul, Türkiye, 2014.

Princess Fahrelnissa Zeid, *Otoportre*,
1988, oil on canvas (*left*) and Sir Anish
Kapoor, *Untitled*, 2013, concave steel
mirror sculpture (*right*). Private *yalı*,
Istanbul, Türkiye, 2014.

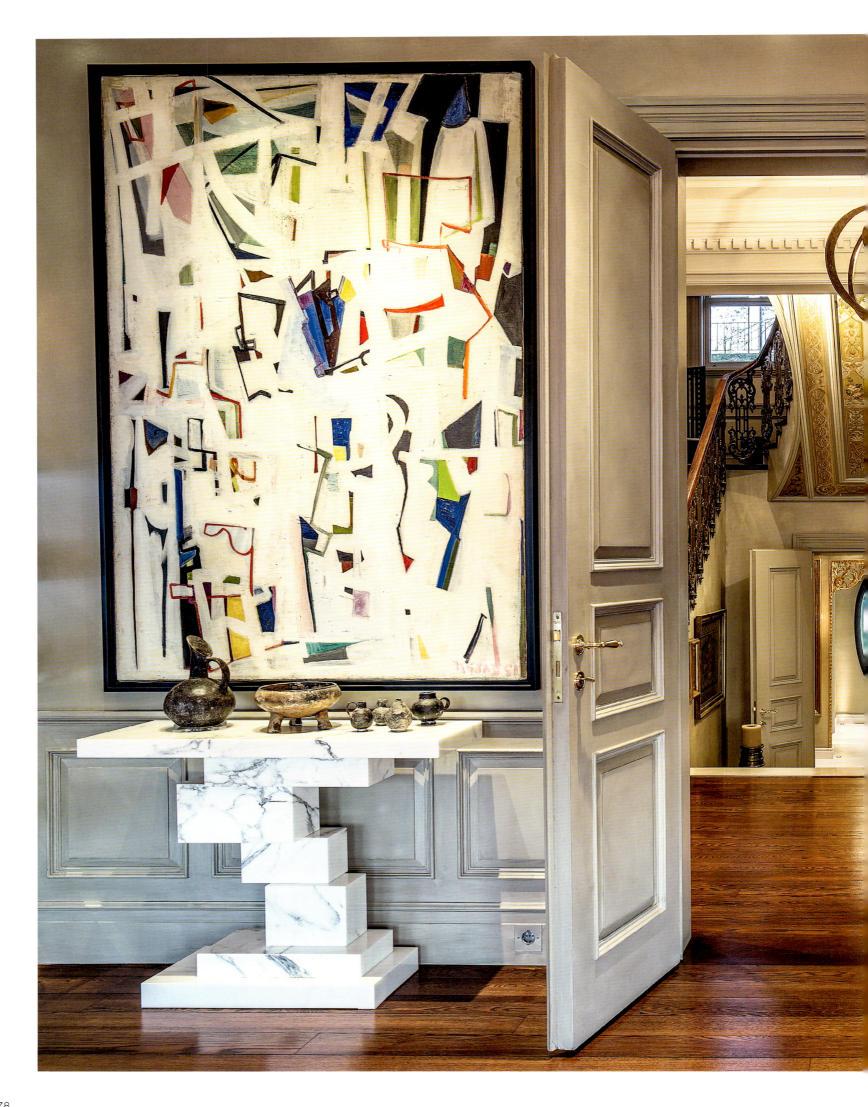

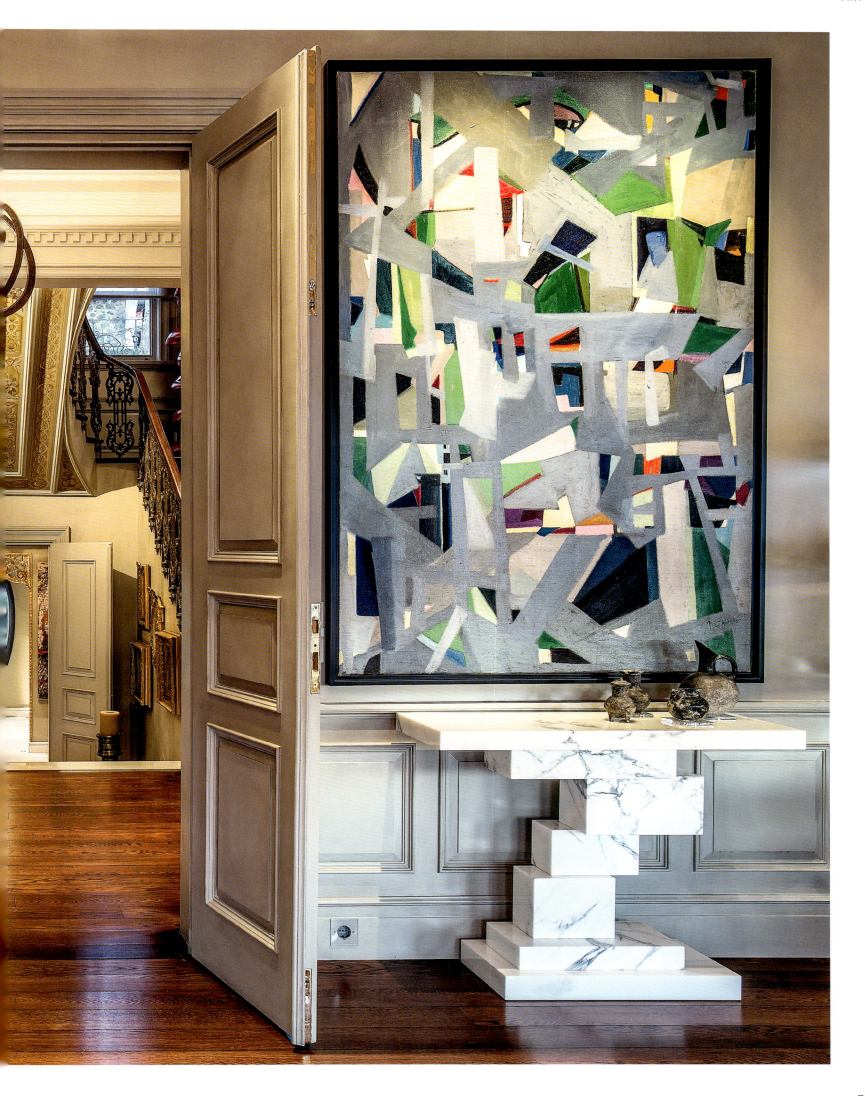

Previous page: Nejad Devrim, *Soyut Kompozisyon (Abstract Composition)*, 1948 and 1950, two oil-on-canvas paintings above geometric marble consoles. Consoles, rock-crystal, and brass chandelier by Hervé Van der Straeten. Beneath the staircase, a hand-painted *kalemişi* (ornamental decoration) mural, gilt architrave from Edirne, and Iván Navarro, *Burden*, 2011, in blue neon, plexiglass, mirror, wood, paint. Private *yalı*, Istanbul, Türkiye, 2014.

Opposite: Thorsten Brinkmann, *Sir Knickrick*, 2012, C-print. Wallpaper by Arte. Wicker Roman shades with *kilim*-inspired interwoven textile borders. Ulus 29 Restaurant Club, Istanbul, Türkiye, c. 2018.

Above: Mustafa Horasan, *Untitled*, 2007, oil on canvas. Ulus 29 Restaurant Club, Istanbul, Türkiye, 2018.

I'll never forget something I saw written on a bridge in Venice during a biennale years ago: "Art doesn't have to be beautiful." These words have remained with me ever since, reminding me that art can be more than just something that is aesthetically inspiring; it can also be about stirring emotions, and sometimes about changing the way we think. Art should have meaning. I have spent a lot of time thinking about where to place art in restaurants for this reason. Something provocative or powerful might fit well at an entrance or in a corridor, but should not be too overwhelmingly close to where one eats. Art should not dominate the experience of dining but it should be part of our lives, not something separate just to be looked at.

When Ulus 29, one of the best-known eating establishments in Istanbul, was designed in 1993, we were the first to install important artworks by famous Turkish artists such as Erol Akyavaş (1932–1999) and Ömer Uluç in a restaurant. People could hardly believe that we dared to combine collectible art that would usually be shown in a gallery or museum with food. I asked an established contemporary painter, İsmail Acar (b. 1971), to decorate the entrance wall. We continued to add to it, so it became a little like an art gallery displaying valuable paintings, video art, and installations. People still take photos of one another in front of the works of art, and from time to time they come back to see what is new.

Similarly, in 2003, in Istanbul's Nişantaşi neighborhood, I arranged artworks in the Nişantaşi Beymen Brasserie restaurant to interact with guests and become a talking point. I worked with Esma Paçal Turam (b. 1963), the Turkish paper sculptor, to install small sculptures of people above the entrance—they appear to be watching and gossiping about the guests. This became the theme for the restaurant, so on one wall we also added *True Legends*, a 3 x 1.5-meter collage by the interior-design company Andrew Martin. Its images of famous people mean that every time you look at it, you recognize someone else. Every change can bring a fresh touch to a space; for example, we recently added custom red, high-gloss, lacquered panels painted by British artist and designer Gordon Levine (b. 1956) to the restaurant, and moved the advertising posters for opera performances at the Munich National Theater, which had been on the back wall, to the inside columns.

Opposite: Onur Gülfidan, *Mercenaries 3*, 2011, oil on canvas. Ulus 29 Restaurant Club, Istanbul, Türkiye, c. 2014.

Next page: Iván Navarro, *Attention*, 2011, neon. Ulus 29 Restaurant Club, Istanbul, Türkiye.

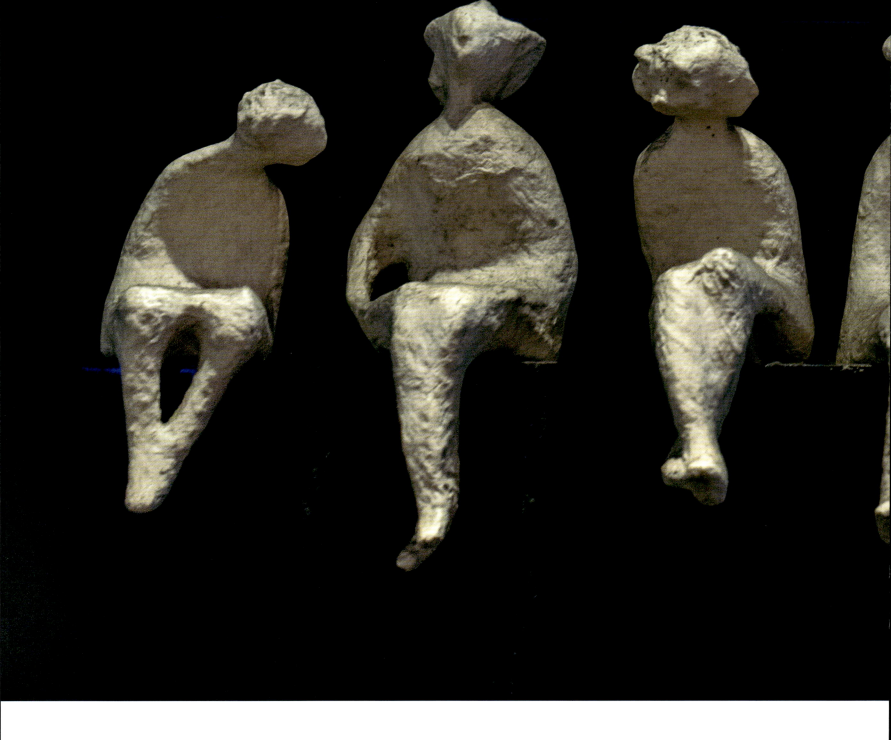

Previous page, left: İsmail Acar, *Sectional Reinterpretation of a Painting by Ingres*, 1993, mural (*center*). Antique pendant by Kalmar (*right*), and *Untitled*, 1993 (*left*). Ulus 29 Restaurant Club, Istanbul, Türkiye.

Previous page, right: Zeynep leans against hand-made tile-clad columns by Italian ceramicists Botteganove. In the background, Ruud van Empel, *World #11*, 2005, photograph. Ulus 29 Restaurant Club, Istanbul, Türkiye, 2018.

This page: Esma Pacal Turam, *The Gossipers*, 2003, papier-mâché. Nişantaşi Beymen Brasserie, Istanbul, Türkiye, 2003.

Previous page: Gordon Levine, *Red City Silhouette*, c. 2023, lacquer, 18 m². Nişantaşi Beymen Brasserie, Istanbul, Türkiye, 2003.

Opposite: Dali-inspired mirror designed by Zeynep, chandelier by Nahide Büyükkaymakçı, and carved wooden bar by Massimo Galimberti. Sinbin Restaurant, Istanbul, Türkiye, 2006.

Above: Trompe-l'oeil sphinx and gold-painted candle arms by glass artist Orhan Koçan, 2006. Sinbin Restaurant, Istanbul, Türkiye, 2006.

Each project has to have its own identity—including art is an effective way to tell a story and to add another layer of influences and meaning to a space; for example, in 2006, we used art to bring a fresh, dramatic dimension to a new restaurant, Sinbin, in the Akmerkez Shopping Mall in Etiler, Istanbul. Taking inspiration from the Surrealists, we installed a large Daliesque mirror that appeared to spill off the wall from the ceiling. Hanging in front of that is an extremely complex crystal chandelier, handcrafted by Turkish artist Nahide Büyükkaymakçi (b. 1963). The Surrealist-style painting in the entrance is also by a local artist, and its unusual psychedelic twist gives diners the impression that they are entering a secret club—a completely different atmosphere to the shopping mall.

In 2015, we designed the interiors of Molu, a chic jewelry boutique in Zorlu Center, an upscale shopping mall in the Beşiktaş district of Istanbul. We had to use the space as efficiently as possible and, because there were many other jewelers nearby, we particularly wanted to make it stand out. We decided to add a sleek, life-size mannequin sculpture created by French interior designer Andrée Putman (1925–2013) for American furniture studio Ralph Pucci. The "performance crafting" touch completely transformed the atmosphere of the boutique and differentiated it from all the adjacent jewelry shops, because the look could very quickly be dramatically transformed by changing the mannequin's clothes and jewelry.

One of my most memorable collaborative artistic experiences was in 2018 in Boston, where we designed the interiors for Nahita (now named Nusr-Et), a Japanese-Peruvian restaurant with a Turkish influence. The monumental scale of the room meant that any paintings hung on the walls would reduce its theatrical impact. I wanted an image to cover the whole back wall, but that would have been prohibitively expensive. Instead, I commissioned a work of art featuring a photograph of a pair of cheetahs by legendary American artist and photographer Peter Beard (1938–2020), which was printed on an enormous backdrop featuring his painting of a wild, intricate medley of animals, insects, plants, and a handwritten quote from Tertullian of Carthage. This three-dimensional collage effect was inspired by *Zara's Tales*, the book of Kenyan stories Peter had written and illustrated for his daughter when she was a child. It was the first time he had produced anything like this, or something on such a large scale, and it was magnificent. When Peter visited the restaurant to see the artwork installed, even he was amazed by its compelling impact—it covered the entire wall. And then, to everyone's delight, he insisted on adding an ink print of his hands. For me, this was not simply about creating a piece of art to hang on the wall, it was about working closely with Peter so that the art would become an integral part of the space.

Opposite: Mannequin by Andrée Putman for Ralph Pucci. Molu Fine Jewelry Shop, Istanbul, Türkiye, 2015.

Peter Beard, *untitled mural*, 2018,
colorprint collage, 6.5 m x 13 m.
Nahita (later renamed Nusr-et),
Boston, United States, 2018.

Art is always essential to the outdoor spaces I create too. In 1987 we commissioned İsmail Acar to paint the canvas ceiling of a Turkish tent that was to be set up outside the Bosphorus waterside restaurant and club Çubuklu 29. His design was a vibrant mix of old and new, contrasting geometric patterns with birds and plants that echoed the surrounding natural landscape.

The club has a 25-meter swimming pool, which became a canvas for one particular artwork. In 2008, we projected a video of a moving butterfly by Turkish-American artist and filmmaker Kutluğ Ataman (b. 1961) onto the surface. Suddenly the water was transformed into a new work of art, and the experience of being at the club changed completely. A pool can sometimes split up an outdoor space, but in this case it became a way to express an original, imaginative energy.

Sometimes art can also add a whimsical touch to an outdoor space. Recently, I found an enormous antique mirror from a lighthouse in an antique shop in Istanbul. I positioned it in a private garden, and it brings a bold, new dimension to the landscape.

Since my taste has changed over the years, in my own home I like mixing several schools of art. I often move things around, juxtaposing old and new, ancient and avant-garde. I'm not a collector in the sense of strategically accumulating items of a particular period or genre, and because of my work I come across so much that is exceptional that I am not driven to own everything I see and love. Instead, I take great pleasure in spending time in galleries, and finding pieces that I know my clients will enjoy.

I tend to find myself working with certain artists and galleries over many years, and we develop long-term relationships. I am usually quite objective about buying art, and I've learned to look, to observe, to walk away, and then to ask myself in what way does it genuinely resonate for me? Then I will still think about it a bit more, read about the piece and the artist to understand it better, and finally decide if I truly want it. This process inevitably means I sometimes lose the chance to buy something—but when I do buy, I know that it's because I consider it really important.

Buying artifacts is a very different thing. When I am inspired by something like a tiny glimpse of color in a tile, or the rare texture of a fabric, or even a coat, I buy it immediately, because I know that I may never find it again. This is the difference between art and crafts for me: the former completes a design and the latter provides endless inspiration. This is why over the years I have been able to develop an archive of wonderful textiles, lacquerware, and ceramics from places as far afield as China, India, Iraq, and Thailand.

Previous page: Peter Beard, *Cheetah Cubs Orphaned at Mweiga nr. Nyeri for The End of the Game*, 1968, photograph with an imprint of the artist's hand in paint. Wall (*right*) features antique sconces and a late seventeenth-century Ottoman banner. Zeynep's home, Istanbul, Türkiye.

Opposite: İnci Eviner, *Friendship*, 2011, acrylic and silkscreen on canvas (*foreground*) and Mehmet İleri, *Don Mehmet*, 1995, oil on canvas (*background*). Antique mid-century daybed reupholstered and repaired. Zeynep's home, Istanbul, Türkiye.

Next page: İnci Eviner, preliminary drawings for video art, 2009 (*left*), and Yoshimoto Nara, *Sleepless Night* figurine, 2007, polystone (*right*). Zeynep's home, Istanbul, Türkiye.

Above: Mehmet Güleryüz, *Untitled*, 1998, oil on canvas (*top*), Charles-Théodore Frère Bey, *Untitled*, 1865, oil on canvas (*bottom*), and "Komet," *Untitled*, 2018, oil on canvas (*corner*). Zeynep's home, Istanbul, Türkiye.

Opposite: John Wragg, *Portrait of Zeynep*, 2018, oil on canvas (*top*). Sèvres vase, 1773, in a niche painted by Antoine (*bottom*). Tayfun Erdoğmuş, two untitled artworks, 2008, mixed media (*left*). Zeynep's home, Istanbul, Türkiye.

Opposite: Louis Gallait, *Portrait*, 1838, oil on canvas. Zeynep's home, Istanbul, Türkiye.

Above: İnci Eviner, two groups of sketches, 2010 and 2011 (*left*) and Salvatore Valeri, *Unknown*, 1886, oil on canvas (*center*). Zeynep's home, Istanbul, Türkiye.

Next page: Design concept for private dining room featuring Iznik-style tiles, mother-of-pearl, and marquetry with a chandelier by Mathieu Lustrerie, Istanbul, 2023.

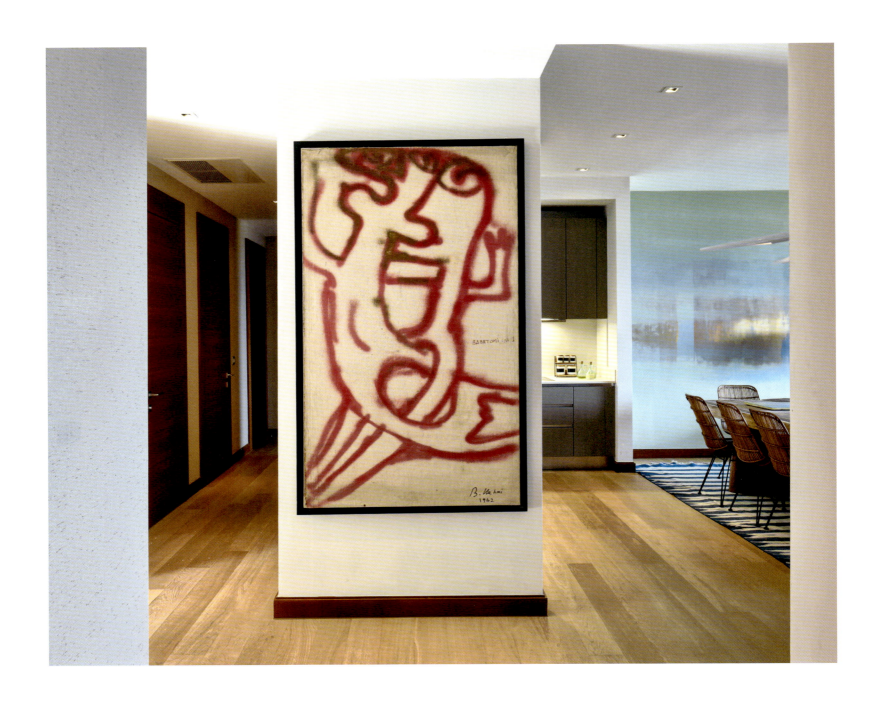

Previous page, left: Ömer Uluç, *Kedi (Cat)* 2005, mixed media on canvas, Ulus 29 Restaurant Club, Istanbul, Türkiye, 2018.

Previous page, right: Julian Opie, *Woman in Sari with Flip-flops*, 2012, vinyl on wooden stretcher. Private residence, Istanbul, Türkiye, 2017.

Above: Bedri Rahmi Eyüboğlu, *Babatomi no: 1*, 1962, oil on canvas. Private residence, Bodrum, Türkiye, 2015.

Opposite: Sabire Susuz, *Olmayan Kadın (Absent Woman)*, 2014, textile labels on fabric (*background*). Pendant from BronzNo5 above vases by Jonathan Adler and table by Carlo. Private residence, Istanbul, Türkiye, 2017.

Left: Princess Fahrelnissa Zeid,
Çerkez Gelin, 1980, oil on canvas.
Polished coconut-shell armchairs by
Carlo. Private residence, Istanbul,
Türkiye, 2017.

I am usually quite objective about
buying art, and I've learned to look,
to observe, to walk away, and then
to ask myself in what way does it
genuinely resonate for me?

Craft

" A true appreciation of beauty cannot be fostered by ignoring practical handicrafts. After all, there is no greater opportunity for appreciating beauty than through its use in our daily lives, no greater opportunity for coming into direct contact with the beautiful. **"**

SOETSU YANAGI[1]

1. "What Is Folk Craft," *The Beauty of Everyday Things* (London: Penguin, 2017) p. 11

Opposite: Friday Mosque, Cultural Village, Katara, Doha, Qatar, 2010. Hand-hammered brass door by Karekin Kaya Kalaycı.

In 2010, when I commissioned master craftsman Karekin Kaya Kalaycı (b. 1959) to hand hammer 3.4-meter-high brass doors for the Friday Mosque in Doha, Qatar, I knew that the beautifully executed layers of detail and tangible natural qualities inspired by Ottoman brass *maşrapa* (water jugs) could provide an aesthetic sensibility, and a strong sense of familiarity for those who pray there.

It is a great responsibility to learn from skills such as these and to keep them alive, and I believe that even the most traditional crafts can be updated in many different ways without losing their intrinsic beauty. The surname Kalaycı means tinsmith and was bestowed on Karekin's grandfather by Mustafa Kemal Atatürk (1881–1938), the founder of modern Türkiye, in recognition of his exceptional metalworking skills. The Armenian family had settled in the Marmara region in the 1600s; they have been experts in this field for generations. Armenian master artisans have always been held in particularly high regard by designers and architects. Despite their declining numbers, globalization, and a digitalized marketplace becoming commonplace, I have always thought it important to source traditional craftspeople such as these, who are open to the opportunity to continue using their skills in a completely new, contemporary context.

In 2006, for instance, I commissioned Recep Ali Serbest Usta (b. 1954), a Turkish master craftsman specializing in casting metals, to create elements for an especially complex sweeping staircase that I had designed together with an artist for Hotel Les Ottomans, Istanbul. The balusters look like elaborate swirling patterns, but are, in fact, calligraphy, and the curved forms took more than six months to make by hand. In 2008, I chose the same craftsman to cast by hand, in iron, another calligraphy-inspired pattern for a glass staircase in a private residence in India. It was a wonderful way to pay homage to the past, while reflecting the client's own taste and individuality.

Previous page, left: Zeynep Fadıllıoğlu Collection metal lantern, screen with cast-metal details, and Fortuny tassel.

Previous page, right: The Peninsula Istanbul, Türkiye, 2023. Geometric patterned ceiling made of aluminum frames and stained glass.

Opposite and next page: Hotel Les Ottomans, Istanbul, Türkiye, 2006. Cast-iron forms inspired by calligraphy on staircase balustrade.

Left: Şakirin Mosque, Istanbul,
Türkiye, 2009. Seljuk-inspired
aluminum mesh facade, 11 m x 20 m.

Another good example of how I've incorporated metalwork into
my designs is through screens. At the modern Ottoman restaurant
Chintamani in London (2002), these were made of ornate ironwork and
perforated sheets of industrial metal; at the Şakirin Mosque in Istanbul
(2009), Seljuk-inspired aluminum mesh facades filter the natural light.
I have also commissioned screens for home interiors from the renowned
French artist Lilou Grumbach-Marquand (b. 1931), who was a close
collaborator of legendary fashion icon Coco Chanel. Elegant metalwork
was combined with traditional Japanese bamboo and *sudare*-inspired
knots and trimmings.

The wonderful thing about metal is that it is so flexible and can be
worked in many different and unusual ways to create even the smallest
of details, from the tips of the legs on my Sini side table or a beautifully
tactile door handle and large architectural pieces.

Ceramics are another subtle way to add bespoke detail and texture
to interiors. This can be particularly impactful in restaurants, where
materiality and tactility are important. For many years now, I have
commissioned ceramics from Gorbon, one of Istanbul's best-known
specialists. The third-generation owner, Orhan Gorbon (b. 1972), has
a keen vision: to invigorate traditional Ottoman patterns for use in
contemporary life. He immediately agreed on the idea when I asked
him to produce an abstract archway for the unique Ottoman-courtyard-
inspired VIP dining room that I had designed for London's Masterpiece
art fair in 2022.

I wanted to break all the rules of traditional design to give a modern take
on Ottoman grandeur, blurring the boundaries of spaces to enhance
continuity between in- and outside, to create lightness and translucence
in a seamless flow of classical and modern styles and periods. The elegant
celadon and deep-burgundy glazed *çini* tiles drop a hint of an arch in
each of the four corners of the room, and are a tribute to the romantic
sensitivity of Ottoman architecture while also being a deconstruction of
the traditional form.

In 2016, at the Fenix Restaurant Club in Bodrum on Türkiye's magical southwest coastline, I designed an outdoor dining area and bar decorated with terra-cotta *saltillo* floor tiles hand made in Mexico. Some bear the footprints of animals as the tiles are left outside to dry. I love the subliminal touch of nature that they bring to the space. On the walls, I added a tropical composition of turquoise, coral, and cobalt-blue tiles arranged in a harlequin pattern, fusing tradition, craft, and nature. I also made a collection of dinnerware with Turkish ceramic artist Meliha Coşkun Tuna (b. 1957) in 2001 for the Keyf-han Restaurant in Istanbul that has interiors by the British architects Nigel Coates (b. 1949) and Doug Branson (b. 1951). The playful, Ottoman-inspired pattern was painted by hand and highlights an interesting interplay between art and craftsmanship.

I often work with glassmakers too. The projects have varied in scale from small pieces, such as the molten-glass, patterned tops of my Çay (tea) side tables made by Turkish glass specialist Orhan Koçan (b. 1963) to monumental ones.

Above: Fenix Restaurant Club, Bodrum, Türkiye, 2016. Multicolored wall tiles in an open-air restaurant and nightclub.

Opposite: Keyf-han Restaurant, Istanbul, Türkiye, 2001. Ceramic plates designed by Meliha Tuna and commissioned by Zeynep Fadıllıoğlu Design.

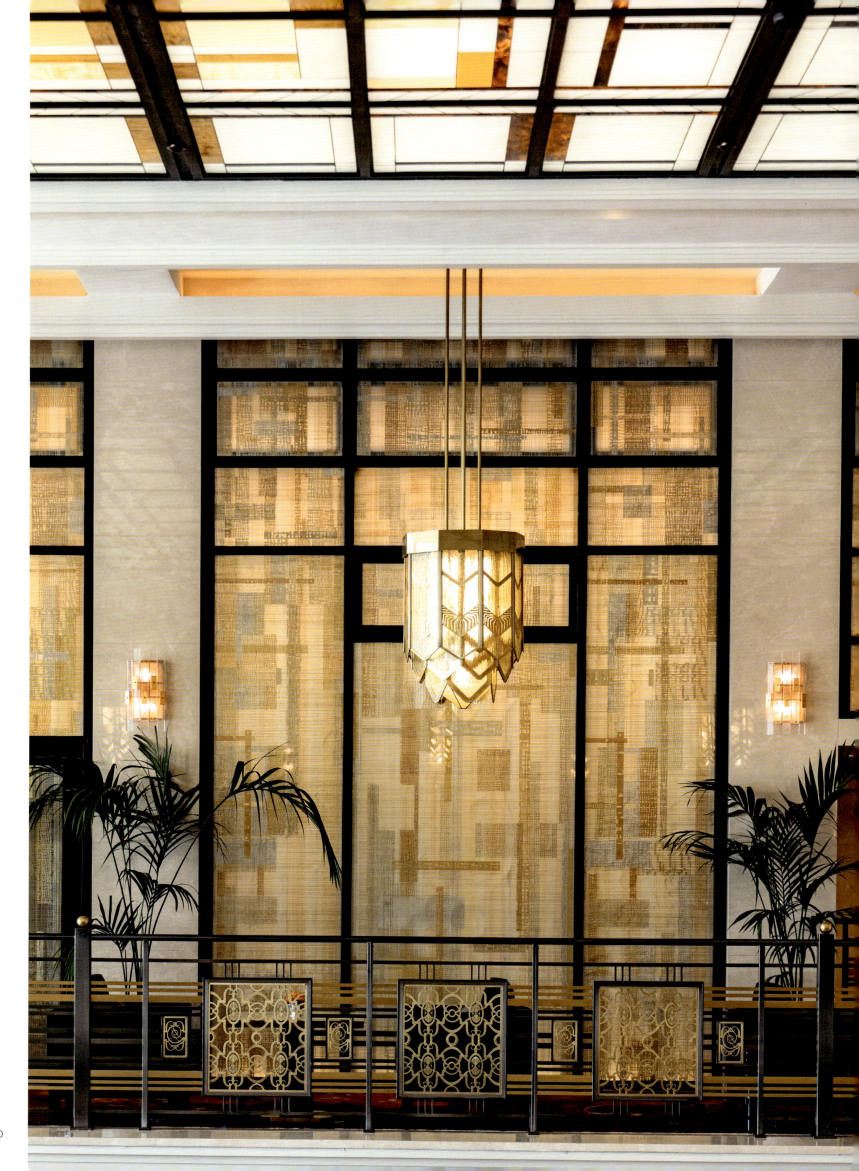

Opposite: Mezzanine of the lobby at The Peninsula Istanbul, Türkiye, 2023. Multilayered engraved, painted glass panels, a collaboration between Zeynep Fadıllıoğlu Design and Kerim Kılıçarslan, and ceiling pendants by Lasvit.

Above: The Peninsula Istanbul ballroom, Türkiye, 2023. Clear, champagne- and amber-colored glass droplets made by Lasvit.

I recently commissioned Czech master glassmakers Lasvit to create eighteen chandeliers that appear like enormous lanterns suspended above the lobby of The Peninsula Istanbul (2023). I didn't want to create a classic light fixture for the Bauhaus building, so instead each lantern comprises three layers of slumped glass—a painstaking process that uses gravity, a mold, and heat from a kiln to shape sheet glass. The process is usually employed when making bowls and platters, but it was worth using it here because the resulting textures are beautiful and impressive—at night, they create a captivating glow. I also designed a pair of sinuous, contemporary chandeliers, each with 811 hand-blown, clear, champagne- and amber-colored glass droplets, for the hotel's ballroom. Each chandelier weighs 2,800 kilograms. In the entrance foyer of the ballroom, I also designed a sculptural arrangement made of glass: 1,005 individual pieces, weighing 3,300 kilograms, were arranged in a lovely curve that appears to float across the ceiling like a cloud.

Left: The lobby of The Peninsula Istanbul, Türkiye, 2023. Detail of a chandelier made by Lasvit with slumped glass layers.

Above: The Peninsula Istanbul, Türkiye, 2023. Developing a material-board palette for the hotel guest rooms.

Opposite: The Peninsula Istanbul, Türkiye, 2023. Blue, gold, and silver geometric-patterned glass sliding doors made by Orhan Koçan (*top*). Bathroom clad with Marmara marble, featuring mother-of-pearl and Alexandra Black marble inlay floors (*bottom*).

The iridescent blue, gold, and silver geometric-patterned glass sliding doors in the guest rooms were made by Orhan Koçan, and transform a purely physical, architectural object into an interactive multidimensional one. The walls of the upper mezzanine of the hotel lobby are encased in shimmering glass panels that were created using layers of engraved glass. The pattern pays homage to the works of German textile artist and printmaker Anni Albers (1889–1994), and was produced in collaboration with Turkish glass artist and academic Kerim Kılıçarslan (b. 1963). The result is that these hand-made panels convey both fragility and durability as well as extraordinary luxury.

The entire lobby ceiling is glass, in a retro color palette featuring an abstract geometric pattern. Originally built in 1940, the building was designed, incidentally, by Orhan Gorbon's grandfather, the eminent architect Rebii Gorbon (1909–1993). Seven hundred square meters of columns and wall panels in the ballroom have been meticulously covered with 16 x 16-centimeter squares of gold leaf, which took four people four months to apply. The effect, both during the day and at night, is magical.

Mosaic is an ancient technique that, despite dating from the third millennium BCE, adds a bold, modern touch to a design when juxtaposed with other materials such as metals. I use mosaics in many different contexts. At The Golden Mosque in Doha (2011), I worked closely with Italian mosaic specialists Sicis to create a glass mosaic that was paired with 24-karat gold leaf to make the interior and exterior appear like a gleaming jewel box, but still able to withstand the dry climate and sandstorms while reflecting Qatar's unique architectural landscape.

Inlay is fast disappearing as a skill, so I do my best to encourage experienced artisans to adapt their traditional methods and work in contemporary ways. For instance, on the Sedir armchair that we designed as part of my Zeynep Fadıllıoğlu Design Collection, launched in 2013, a slender line of birch was added to a traditional walnut wood base to reflect light in an interesting way. In the Maldives, we designed a contemporary television cabinet inlaid with different seashells for a hospitality project (2015), while for the Friday Mosque (2018) in Manama, Bahrain, the *mihrab* (a niche that shows the direction in which Muslims must pray) and cabinets are in a number of varying inlaid materials: two different tones of wood, mother-of-pearl, and semi-transparent shells backed with gold leaf. Although the techniques used were traditional, the innovative pattern gives them a contemporary feel.

Right: Golden Mosque, Cultural Village, Katara, Doha, Qatar, 2011. Gold-leaf glass mosaic made by Italian specialist Sicis.

Left: Concept sketch for a hospitality project, Maldives, 2015.

Next page, left: Zeynep Fadıllıoğlu Collection Sedir chair and Zigon side tables, both with wooden marquetry.

Next page, right: Inlay detail of Zeynep's grandmother's antique folding chair. Personal collection.

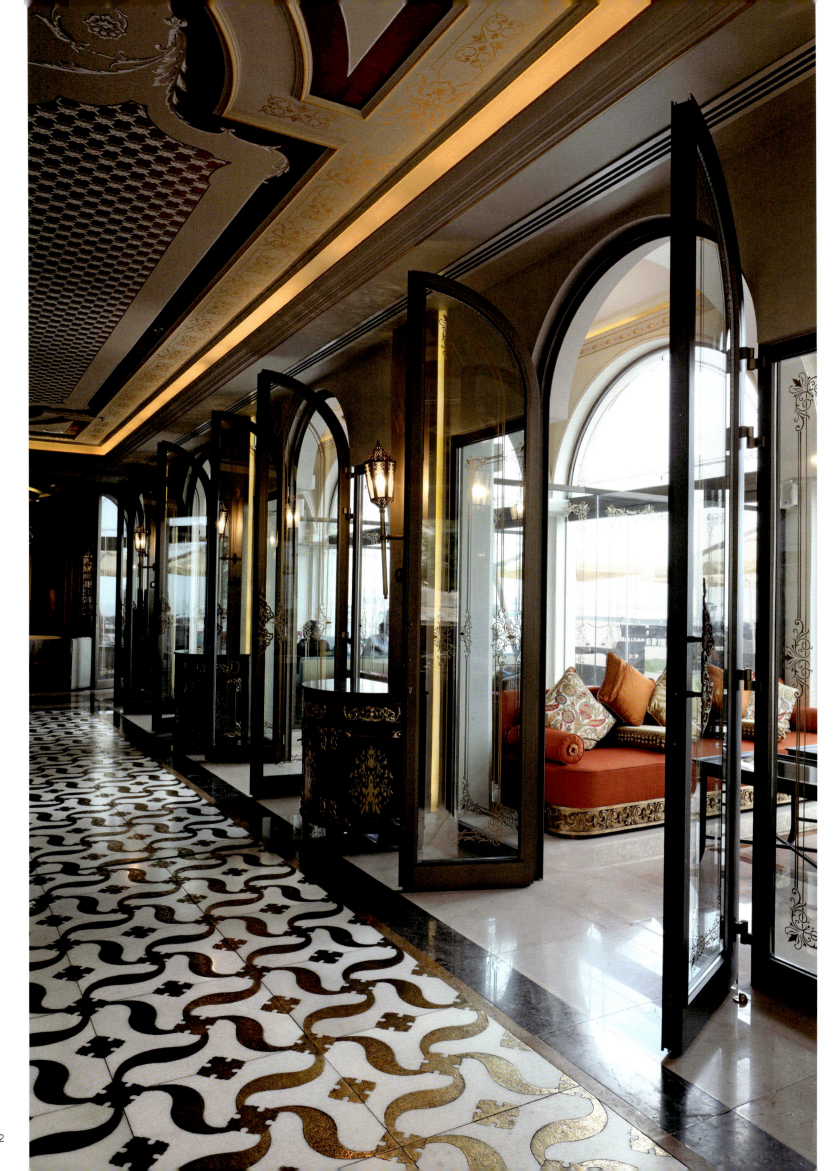

Opposite: Sukar Pasha Ottoman Lounge, Cultural Village, Katara, Doha, Qatar, 2011. Stone and inlay hammered-brass floor by Steve Charles.

Stonework is part of daily life in Türkiye. Its decorative use dates from the eleventh century, when Seljuk nomads decided to create a permanent home in Anatolia and began to carve fine architectural elements from stone, mainly in high relief. Turkish marble is elegant and hard-wearing, and what you can do with it is incredible. To me, the most exciting thing is when, as a designer, one can also be a catalyst, pushing the limits of a material. For instance, in 2011 in Qatar, working with surface specialist Steve Charles (b. 1951), we designed a stone and hammered-brass floor with different finishes for the Sukar Pasha Ottoman Lounge, weaving traditional Islamic architecture and culture into the interiors. A year later, for the modern Ottoman-style Martı Hotel Taksim in Istanbul (2012), I commissioned a counter carved from marble and quartzite, with geometric details inspired by late fifteenth-century ornamentation on the exterior wall of Has Oda, at Istanbul's Topkapı Palace.

Materiality is also very important to me; I've always loved using different textures to add a new dimension to a space. I especially enjoy sourcing unusual handmade fabrics, and I also design textiles myself.

At Masterpiece London (2022), I flanked an eighteenth-century Franconian gilt console table with a trio of columns. I also displayed my Sedir Mini lounge chair (2022), wrapped in antique textiles from my own private collection, placed on a handmade wall-to-wall carpet by rug specialists Stepevi from southern Türkiye. The rug, which we designed, is a modern-day version of a *kilim*, and the burgundy section of the carpet, which forms the background, is "cut" to emphasize the beige loops.

Above: Six Senses Kocataş Mansions, Istanbul, Türkiye, 2019. Bathroom with Marmara marble.

Opposite: The Peninsula Istanbul, Türkiye, 2023. Marmara marble cut in *muqarnas*-inspired shapes on an alcove at the entrance to the spa.

Opposite and next page, left: Friday Mosque, Cultural Village, Katara, Doha, Qatar, 2010. Columns clad in leather and handcrafted metal.

Next page, right: Friday Mosque, Cultural Village, Katara, Doha, Qatar, 2010. Glass chandelier.

I also enjoy using leather in my designs. In 2010, at the Friday Mosque in Doha, I sheathed columns in this versatile material adding a subtle nod to traditional Islamic craftsmanship. At the Martı Hotel Taksim, and Bali Hotel, Bali (2015), I used leather for straps on canvas blinds, suggestive of the Turkish house shutters, for an outdoor pavilion.

Craft is not just about preserving tradition; it is also about the future—the avant-garde and innovation—and there have been many times where blending digital crafts and artisanal skills have enabled me to extend the possibilities of design. For example, at the Martı Hotel Taksim, we digitally printed an antique Ottoman textile motif onto canvas, and then displayed this behind glass panels in the hotel lobby. In 2017 in Qatar, digital manipulation of drawings proved invaluable when we wanted to produce an exquisite painted effect on a canvas ceiling that we had suspended inside a 2,000-square-meter Ottoman-inspired Ramadan tent made of concrete. Computerization allowed us to create something outstanding in a complex setting that would have been almost impossible to do entirely by hand within a very tight time frame.

I believe design is the only way to keep handicrafts alive, and we need to remember that this is about much more than drawing on aesthetics: it's about maintaining our cultural heritage. Even when budget is a constraint, I try to add detail to my designs through crafts so that there is still a story to tell—a patina, an additional layer of meaning to each project. Often, it is only when a client touches a handmade object that they fully understand the value of the craftsmanship. It is my responsibility as a designer to demonstrate to both clients and craftspeople that there are endless exciting, interesting, and contemporary opportunities for these age-old techniques.

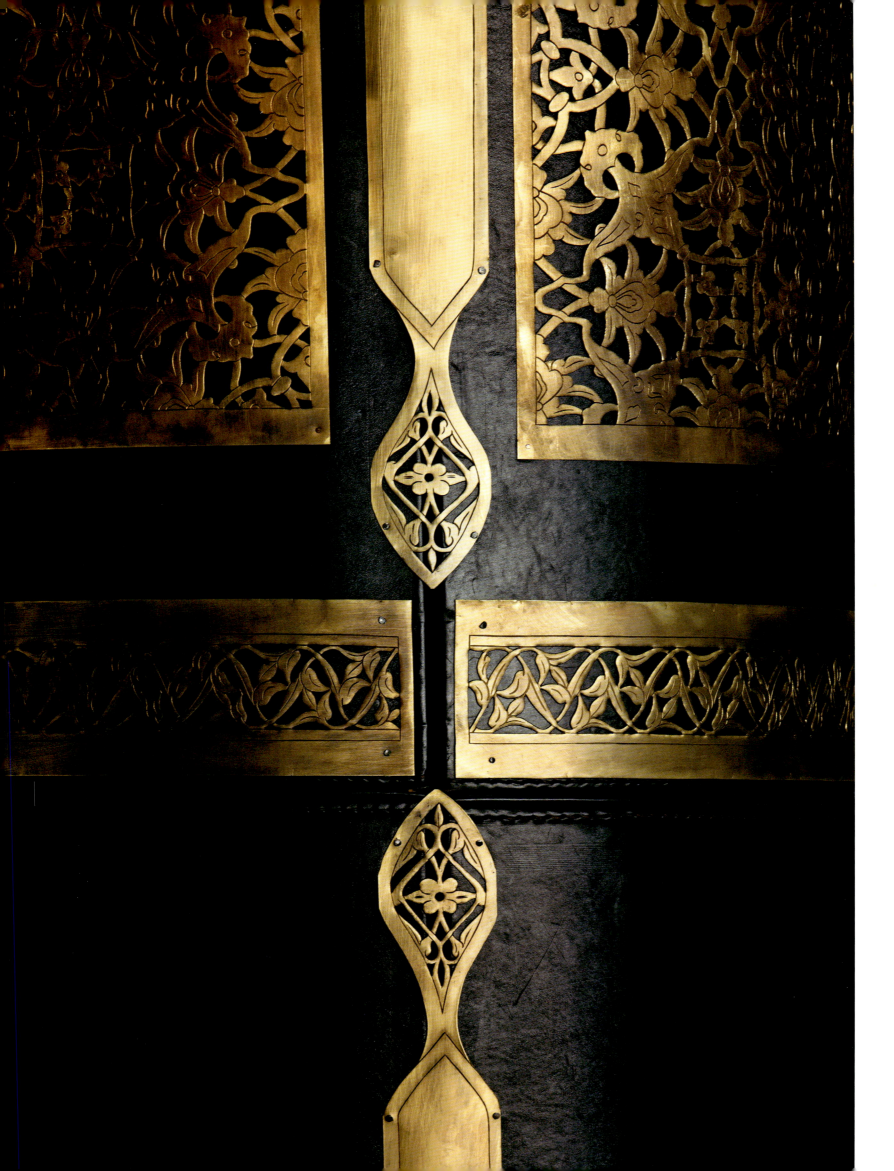

Previous pages, left and right: Nişantaşi Beymen Brasserie, Istanbul, 2003. A 1930s Murano glass chandelier. It illuminates a custom-made glass tabletop by Orhan Koçan.

Left: Ulus 29, İstanbul, Turkiye, c. 2011. Swarovski crystal chandelier design by Zeynep Fadıllıoğlu, created by Nahide Büyükkaymakçı.

Next page, left: Zeynep Fadıllıoğlu Collection Koni cocktail table. Glass made by Orhan Koçan.

Next page, right: Private residence, Bodrum, Türkiye, 2015. Art Deco antique sconce with glass details, displayed against mural by Gordon Levine.

Page 156: Zeynep at work.

Page 157: Zeynep Fadıllıoğlu Collection Çay side tables with glass by Orhan Koçan.

Previous pages: Glass surface of
Fadıllıoğlu Collection Çay side tables.

Left: Private residence, Istanbul,
Türkiye, 1999. Matching pair of Lilou
Grumbach-Marquand-style metal
screens with Fortuny glass pendant
light at the center.

Next page, left: Private mansion,
Tarabya, Istanbul, Türkiye, 2015.
Metal door with timber inlay details.

Next page, right: Golden Mosque,
Doha, Qatar, 2011. Brass *mihrab*
with hammered and embossed
cursive script.

Above: Private mansion, Bosphorus,
Istanbul, Türkiye, 2006. M Belloni,
The Harem Favorite, c. 19th century,
oil on canvas. Mother-of-pearl *kakma*
inlaid wall cabinetry. Eser-i Istanbul
antique console with Beykoz glasswork
and curule chair. Fuschia cushion
with an antique textile on a Rubelli-
upholstered daybed.

Above: Hotel Les Ottomans,
Istanbul, Türkiye, 2006. Trompe-
l'oeil hand-painted concrete walls
and ceiling, reminiscent of a
traditional Ottoman tent.

Above: The lobby, Hotel Les
Ottomans, Istanbul, Türkiye, 2006.
Ottoman-style *sebil* cascading
fountains with classical colonnades.
Embroidered textile with inset
mirror. Daybed by Zeynep Fadıllıoğlu
Design. Reproduction of chandelier
in Dolmabahçe Palace.

Opposite: Ulus 29 Restaurant Club,
Istanbul, Türkiye, 2011. Fabrics draped
across a ceiling evoke Ottoman-style
tent interiors.

Left: Private residence, Istanbul, Türkiye, 2016. Glass-clad column with oxidized brass-plate cutout corner made by artist Orhan Koçan.

Craft is not just about preserving tradition; it is also about the future— the avant-garde and innovation.

Heritage

> **❝** I have great respect for the past. If you don't know where you've come from, you don't know where you're going. **❞**

MAYA ANGELOU[1]

1. Randy Cordova, "Interview," *Arizona Republic*, originally published 2011, see: https://www.azcentral.com/story/entertainment/books/2014/05/28/maya-angelou-arizona-republic-interview/9682587/ (accessed 23 May 2023).

Previous page, left: The Peninsula Istanbul, Türkiye, 2023. Guest suite 100-percent wool, hand-tufted carpet made by Tai Ping.

Previous page, right: Osman Hamdi Bey, *Two Musician Girls*, 1880, oil on canvas. Suna and İnan Kıraç Foundation.

Opposite: Eighteenth-century fez embroidered with a geometric pattern of silver-gilt thread. Bought from Aleppo antique bazaar, Syria. Zeynep's personal collection.

Above: Clay figures and pottery. Twelfth-century Seljuk and Turkic roots. Zeynep's personal collection.

Next page, left: İznik çini tile. Mid-seventeenth century. Sadberk Hanım Museum.

Next page, right: The Peninsula Istanbul, Türkiye, 2023. Tiled alcove of the staff dining room; tiles by Gorbon.

Turkish heritage has always been a distinct part of my identity and inspiration. I try to look at the past with fresh eyes, though, and do not let it hold me back, because to me respecting heritage and traditions doesn't mean copying or being confined by yesterday.

I am fortunate to have been raised in a home influenced by many different cultures, because my parents and grandparents had eclectic tastes and collected art from around the world. Our waterside home in Yeniköy, which has a pair of monumental staircases and a seven-meter-high ceiling in the living room, was created in the 1850s by the famous architect Garabet Balyan (1800–1866), who also designed the Dolmabahçe Palace. My grandparents decorated our *yalı* with European furnishings and artifacts—from Sèvres and Meissen porcelain to Fabergé. I particularly remember the glittering Victorian chandeliers and our Pleyel double grand piano. We would regularly visit flea markets and antique shops in Istanbul and abroad, but at that time we tended to take the Turkish art and crafts that surrounded us for granted, preferring international art and design.

It is ironic that I first became truly aware of the richness of my cultural heritage after I left Istanbul in 1978 to study at the Inchbald School of Design in London. We attended classes in art and design at the Victoria and Albert Museum (V&A), and I was impressed by the deep respect accorded to Türkiye's rich cultural heritage, in particular to ceramics and rugs. I think a degree of separation heightens one's appreciation of heritage, and in my case it sharpened my eyes to details that I had overlooked.

For instance, I only became aware of the importance of tiles made in İznik in northwest Anatolia after reading a fascinating V&A exhibition catalog and visiting the museum's own superlative ceramics collection. This was a defining moment for me, because until then I had not appreciated the astonishing variety and detail of this ancient art and, even though the tiles decorated the walls of mosques and palaces in Istanbul, few individuals collected them.

In London, I was intrigued to learn about the evolution of the complex decorative patterns and colors of Iznik ware from early examples that copied blue-and-white Chinese porcelain to the innovative color palettes used at the Süleymaniye Mosque in Istanbul, which was built between 1550 and 1557. The potters, who had originally worked only with cobalt blue, now included red, turquoise, pink, and green glazes, and an unmistakably Ottoman repertoire of enchanting floral designs.

I started collecting very slowly, and I still have the pieces I bought many years ago. Iznik ware has been an inspiration for many of my projects. For example, an ethereal floral composition on an Iznik plate at the Sadberk Hanım Museum in Istanbul provided inspiration for my modern interpretation of tiles made by Gorbon for a 5.8 x 2.8-meter alcove in The Peninsula Istanbul (2023) staff dining room. The decorative motif, called Hatai because it was brought to Anatolia by the Hatay Turks from Central Asia, is also known as Ottoman chinoiserie and widely used in the decoration of carpets and tiles. The style is distinctive for its elegance. Also at The Peninsula Istanbul, *Lady Taurus* (2022), a matching pair of stunning navy and white ceramic-tile sculptures by Ankara-born artist Elif Uras (b. 1972), is a contemporary nod to Iznik ceramics. It provides a striking contrast to the dramatic, three-dimensional, geometric, Marmara marble mosaic, inspired by modernized *muqarnas* forms, that I designed for the wall behind it.

While I was studying in London, I also learned about Turkish textiles, and was delighted to recognize patterns and motifs that I had seen on the clothes my grandmothers wore. Themes such as animals, flowers, and fruit have been used in Turkish fabrics, carpets, and the decorative arts for centuries—and many have auspicious meanings that, interpreted in a fresh context, establish a link between past and present. The pomegranate, a symbol of prosperity, is an excellent example of this, and has an important religious and cultural significance. Over the years, I have also found myself drawn to intricate floral designs, some of which look remarkably modern and abstract.

Page 180: Heirloom hand-embroidered antique towel. Zeynep's personal collection.

Page 181: Early twentieth-century French ottoman upholstered with gold-gilt threaded silk, resting on an antique Persian carpet and natural sisal rug. Zeynep's personal collection.

Previous pages, left and right: The Peninsula Istanbul, Türkiye, 2023. Ballroom with Tree of Life carpet designed by Zeynep Fadıllıoğlu Design and made by Tai Ping.

Left: Elif Uras, *Lady Taurus*, 2022, ceramic. Artwork collaboration with curator Çağla Saraç. The Spa at The Peninsula Istanbul, Türkiye, 2023.

Next page, left: The Peninsula Istanbul, Türkiye, 2023. Metal balustrade with dark-bronze and satin-brass finishes. Burgundy carpet with turquoise and ochre accents.

Next page, right: The Peninsula Istanbul, Türkiye, 2023. Lobby lounge area with bespoke furniture and lighting fixtures designed by Zeynep Fadıllıoğlu Design.

I became so intrigued by Turkish rugs that I wrote my thesis on this handicraft during the Seljuk and Ottoman periods. I was fascinated by how a rug's designs and hues could reflect different regions as well as beliefs and practices. For example: a hooked shape represents a burdock, a plant with burrs, which is thought to fend off the Evil Eye, and a ram's horn signifies power and bravery. Ever since, whenever I design a rug or floor covering, such as the one made for the ballroom of The Peninsula Istanbul, I look to create a harmony between craftsmanship, materiality, and symbolism.

The rug in The Peninsula Istanbul ballroom measures 39.6 x 20.1 meters and its pattern includes a number of ancient motifs, including my twenty-first-century take on the Tree of Life, which has a strong philosophical and religious resonance across many different cultures. We chose a classic rich burgundy color for the lobby carpet, because the design hinted at Ottoman motifs with its floral pattern of elegant swooping curves in harmonious proportions, but it is actually quite modern. It was made by Hong Kong–based carpet company Tai Ping, and is an artistic reflection of another culture steeped in history and heritage.

For centuries, calligraphy has been an important art form in the Islamic world, and I have always been fascinated as much by its expressive and abstract qualities as its poetry. I often look to introduce calligraphy in my designs through different mediums—from stone and marble to glass and wood or leather—infusing the gentle dynamism of its centuries-old ornamental forms with a modern sensibility. At the Golden Mosque in Doha (2011), for instance, my modern interpretation of a very minimal and beautifully composed Qur'anic verse, originally created by the Ottoman calligrapher Ahmed Şemseddin Karahisârî (1468–1566) in 1550, is presented in brass inlaid on marble. The *mihrab* features cursive script hand hammered in embossed brass.

I think handcrafts are central to cultural identity: making, shaping, and molding objects—by hand—influences the development of their aesthetics, symbolic forms, and patterns. One reason I welcome the opportunity to work with different materials, from silk and ceramics to wood, is that their historical elements add the value of sustainability to an object, but also a modern meaning. The challenge is how to avoid indulging in cultural nostalgia—sometimes just a hint is enough.

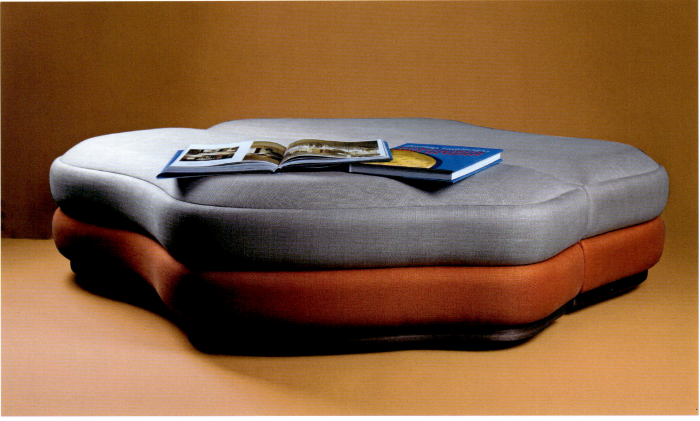

Previous page, left: The Peninsula Istanbul, Türkiye, 2023. Maple and walnut inlay on burl walnut-topped nest of cocktail tables; hand-tufted tone-on-tone grey-beige carpet by Tai Ping, inspired by traditional Uşak rug bird motif.

Previous page, right: Golden Mosque, Doha, Qatar, 2011. Brass inlay and pietra dura technique on marble, calligraphy inspired by Ahmet Karahisari.

Above: Zeynep Fadıllıoğlu Design Collection Kubbe oak tray on a Sandık Chest (*top*). Zeynep Fadıllıoğlu Design Collection Ada pouf (*bottom*).

In my range of furniture and accessories (the Zeynep Fadıllıoğlu Design Collection, 2013), for example, the Memo table evokes traditional folding tables and trays, yet also gives a modern cut to the shape, fine detail, and approach to finishes. The suggestion of classic floral forms and colors in my Ada pouf—a quirky name, as *ada* means island in Turkish—adds depth and authenticity to the latest interiors, something that I believe people instinctively recognize has been used elsewhere. The Kubbe tray is reminiscent of the old-fashioned metal trays carried by men delivering tea in Moroccan and Egyptian markets; my interpretation is handmade in Türkiye of walnut or oak, and is unmistakably contemporary.

Previous page: Zeynep at Maison&Objet Fair, Paris, France, 2013.

Above: Zeynep Fadıllıoğlu Design Collection Memo traditional folding table.

Above: The Peninsula Istanbul, Türkiye, 2023. Traditional shadow puppets, pictured here the characters Karagöz and Hacivat, displayed behind glass panels in the staff dining room.

Designing so many restaurants early in my career gave me a unique opportunity to experiment with everything from architecture to arts and crafts and materials. I never design to create a picture; I design for a space to be lived in, and that is a very, very important difference. That discipline has stayed with me, so when I design on a much larger scale with heritage constraints, I always try to think about what the people who will be using the space will need.

In the staff dining room of The Peninsula Istanbul, a heritage property, I installed a wall along a corridor featuring traditional paper shadow-theater puppets, which add a fresh, unexpected, and whimsical link to our cultural past. Traditional storytellers would use puppets to entertain patrons in coffee houses, so the connection to the present-day dining room feels relevant.

Fait par Ignaz Melling i...

Left: Antoine Ignace Melling, *View of Istanbul from the Galata Tower*, 1787, watercolor on paper, 56.5 x 74.5 cm. Suna and İnan Kıraç Foundation.

Right: Antalya 29 Restaurant Club, Antalya, Türkiye, 1987. A popular jet-set venue with restaurant, nightclub, and beach club. Hardscape created from salvaged stone masonry to respect the heritage of the surrounding area.

Next page: Chintamani Restaurant, London, UK, 2002. Eleventh-century Khorasan-style-finished walls by artist Hülya Yıldırım (b. 1957); tented ceilings; wicker dining chairs with silk, taffeta, and velvet accents.

At the Chintamani Restaurant in London (2002), I combined multiple references to Ottoman cultural heritage with modern comfort, adding low tables; low-slung, comfortable sofas; and felted, tented ceilings that were slashed in a style reminiscent of the cut paintings of Argentine-Italian artist Lucio Fontana (1889–1968) and made by Turkish multimedia artist Selçuk Günışık (b. 1954). Walls were rough-finished and inset with glass discs, inspired by the eleventh-century Khorasan style of plaster typical of traditional domed hammam ceilings. I also outfitted the restaurant's luxurious contemporary bathrooms with traditional Turkish marble sinks. Handcrafted bronze *mashrabiya* are reminiscent of Ottoman-style wooden window screens.

I feel comfortable about looking at all cultural heritages from different perspectives. When I work in another country, and with a different lifestyle, I am aware that we must understand its past to be able to refer to it in a complimentary way—through colors or textures, for example. Often the history of a place, or culture, has many different facets, from myths and legends to religions. When I am designing, I like to spend time trying to understand what has gone before, adding my own dimension.

For instance, in Türkiye the architecture and interior arrangement of mosques are still influenced by the sixteenth-century Ottoman architect Sinan (c. 1488–1588). Yet when I designed the Şakirin Mosque in Istanbul (2009), I was able to sensitively conceptualize the architecture in a new way, while staying true to heritage principles. Natural light is usually uniform throughout the interior of a mosque; however, my facade filters daylight, creating a wonderful sense of tranquility. I elevated the women's prayer space, and installed a beautiful bronze-and-plexiglass chandelier with blown-glass "raindrops," to create a particularly pleasing view of the *mihrab*.

Sometimes honoring heritage is about showing that old and new, traditional and innovative can live side-by-side in harmony. Ottoman hammams are a good source of inspiration and a model for this. My studio was the first to design stylish contemporary bathrooms that hint at the aesthetics and ambience of these traditional bathhouses, which were typically magnificent and grand in size because they provided a cultural hub, a meeting place where people could relax and socialize. When we translate this sensibility into a modern home, I aim to create timelessness and familiarity, as well as a feeling of grandeur, even if it is in a relatively small, private space like a bathroom.

Page 200: Princes' Islands, Istanbul, Türkiye, 2017. Marmara marble walls, sinks, and tabletop at a boutique hotel and clubhouse.

Page 201: The Peninsula Suite, The Peninsula Istanbul, Türkiye, 2023. Hammam with Carrara marble and Iznik tiles made by the İznik Foundation.

Previous pages: The Peninsula Istanbul, Türkiye, 2023. Modern hammam featuring Marmara marble-clad walls, basins, benches, and navel stone.

Right: Private yalı, Istanbul, Türkiye, 2014. Powder room with mirrored cabinets and video artwork of Bosphorus tides by Kutluğ Ataman. Golden glass tiles by Steve Charles. Antique kurna with tap. Vanity chair and side table by Mark Brazier-Jones, Baccarat sconces, and Marmara marble floor.

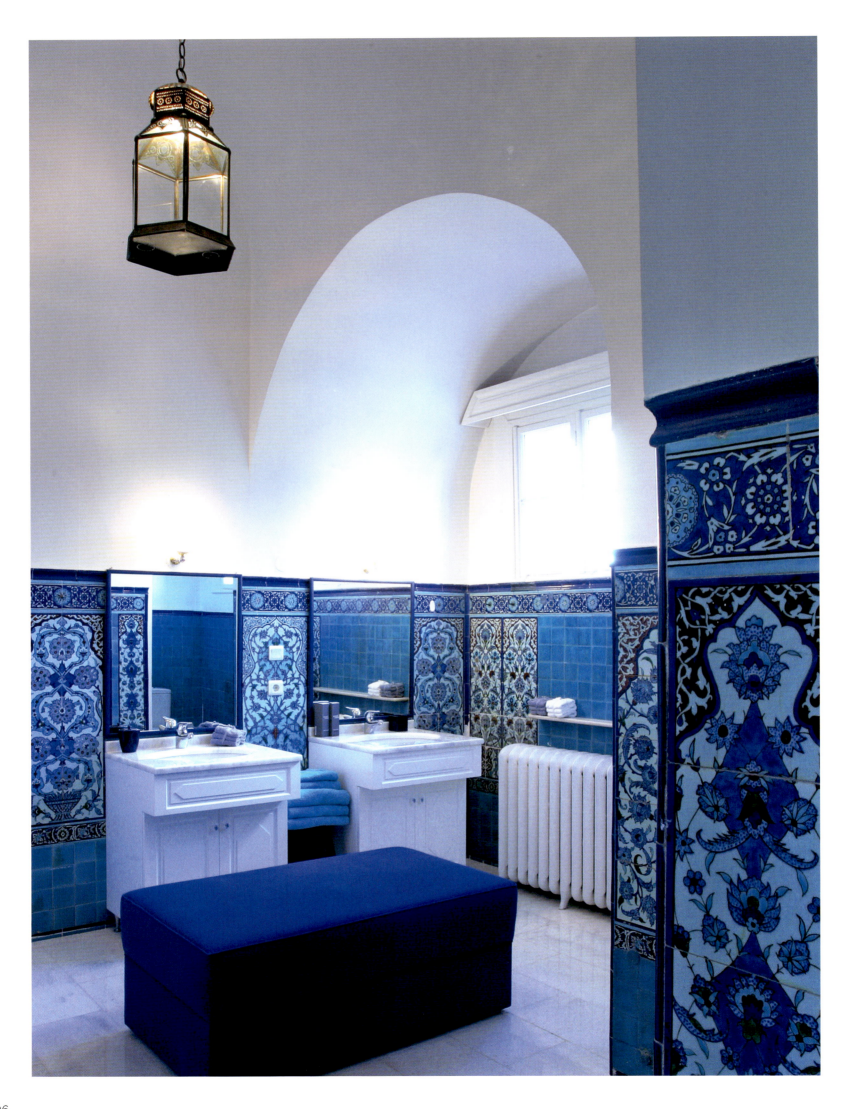

Opposite: Private residence, Istanbul 2008. Bathroom featuring restored late nineteenth-century tiles, originally created for the Ottoman military officer, Enver Pasha.

Above: Hotel Les Ottomans, Istanbul, Türkiye, 2006. Metal-mesh enclosure, inspired by Iznik tiles.

Next page, left: Eighteenth-century hand-carved Indian marble, and horsehair fly-flap. Zeynep's private collection.

Next page, right: Eleventh-century iron oil lamp. Zeynep's private collection.

A good example of this is the serene, minimalist bathroom that I designed in 2008 for a private villa in the Arnavutköy district of Istanbul. It had distinctive blue tiles and a domed ceiling reminiscent of a traditional Turkish bathhouse. In the same year, I designed the brand concept and boutiques for the bath-product shop Hammam in Istanbul. I took inspiration from the high wooden clogs traditionally worn in hammams to protect the wearer from soapy water and created a striking entrance. The clogs were typically embellished with precious metals, or inlaid with mother-of-pearl or tortoise-shell, and featured embroidered or bejeweled leather straps. They could be as high as 30 centimeters, and the quality of the craftsmanship reflected the bather's status. I translated this relationship into the design of a contemporary entranceway, setting the scene for an especially luxurious experience.

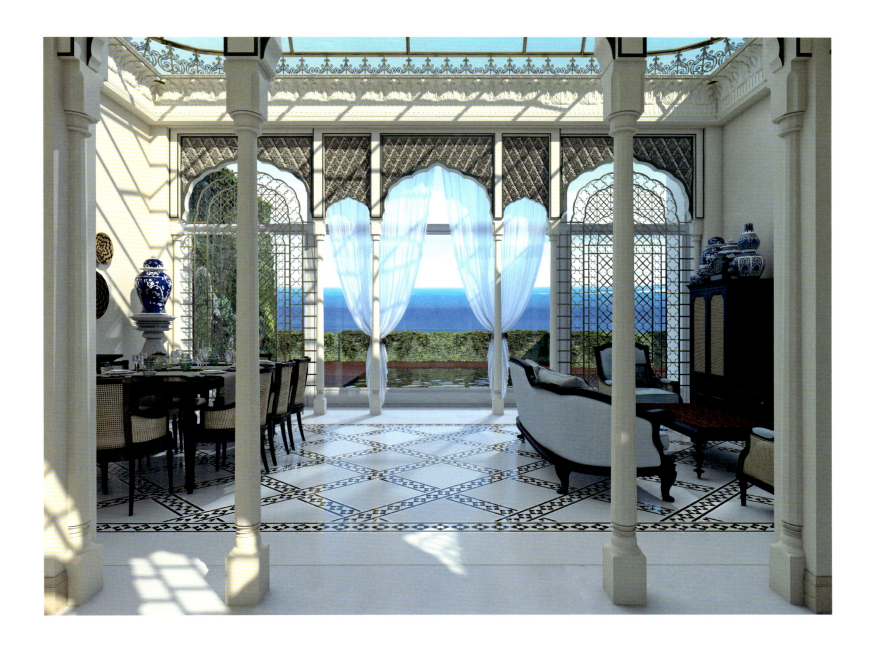

Previous page, left: Six Senses
Kocataş Mansions, Istanbul, Türkiye,
2019. Marble-clad, custom-painted
bathroom, "Cistern" guest room.

Previous page, right: Hotel Les
Ottomans, Istanbul, Türkiye, 2006.
Hand-painted *kalemişi* niche.

Left: Berna Bal, Tent-form Pavilion,
2023, Illustration inspired by
nineteenth-century work by Johann
Gottfried Grohmann.

Above: Cultural Village, Katara,
Doha, Qatar, 2017. Concept-design
rendering for a boutique hotel.

Right: Fabrics, including early twentieth-century Mariano Fortuny (dark teal), and seventeenth- and eighteenth-century Ottoman textiles. Zeynep's personal collection.

Next page, left: Zeynep's home, Istanbul, Türkiye. Antique Ottoman extended sofa with Japanese textiles and Mirella Spinella Venetian cushion. Zeynep Fadıllıoğlu Design Collection Çay side table.

Next page, right: Clubhouse, Princes' Islands, Istanbul, Türkiye, 2017. Ottoman-style divan, with golden and patinated valances.

Above and right: Six Senses Kocataş
Mansions, Istanbul, Türkiye, 2019:
a restored and renovated heritage
building. On this page, a corridor lined
with framed Ottoman miniatures. On
the opposite page, a bedroom featuring
bespoke brass bed frame and Zeynep
Fadıllıoğlu Design Collection Sandık chest.

Left: The VIP dining room of the Masterpiece Art Fair, London, 2022. *Topkapı* hand-painted custom design on tarnished silver gilded paper, a collaboration with de Gournay.

Sometimes honoring heritage is about showing that old and new, traditional and innovative can live side-by-side in harmony.

Narrative

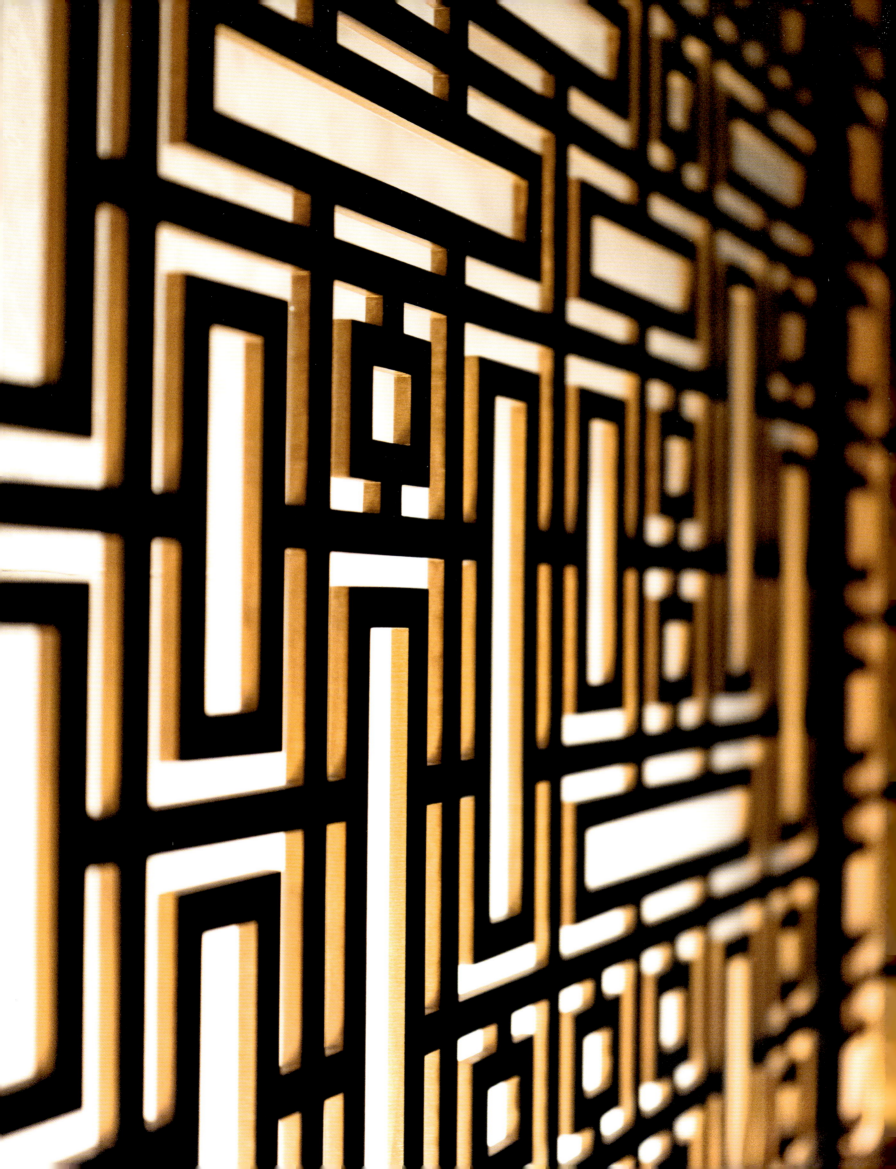

" A plan calls for the most active imagination. It calls for the most severe discipline also. The plan is what determines everything; it is the decisive moment. **"**

LE CORBUSIER[1]

Opposite: The Peninsula Istanbul, Türkiye, 2023. Satinated brass screens inspired by *kündekari*, a traditional geometric woodwork technique.

Next pages: Antoine Ignace Melling, *Kahvehane (Coffee House)*, etching from *Voyage Pittoresque de Constantinople et rives de Bosphore*, (Paris, Treuttel et Würtz, 1819), p. 32.

1. Le Corbusier, *Towards a New Architecture* (US: BN Publishing, 2008), p. 48

Our design studio is known for its use of color and materials, textures, and bespoke art and furniture, but the one thing that unites these elements—and adds something new—is storytelling.

The process of developing a narrative for an interior is similar to the way an author might write a novel: details are woven together to build profiles of characters and settings that produce unique atmospheres and experiences as each scene unfolds. Very few clients come to a designer with a blank page. However, it's important for us to remember that we are not designing for ourselves, so we listen as much to what individuals don't say about their vision for a space as to what they do, because sometimes reading between the lines is where the opportunity for true creativity lies.

I like to think that I am as practical as I am creative, and my emphasis on rationality in our designs probably stems from my early passion for mathematics and computing. I don't see practicality and creativity as mutually exclusive. A narrative is a creative tool that can be used to set a framework for both efficiency and inventiveness in a design. It often raises important questions about a project, and this means you have a better chance of addressing them. While artistic sensibility will make interiors engaging, for example, one must also be pragmatic, and consider how the spaces will be used now and in the future.

A storyline helps our clients to understand the importance of individual details and how they work together to create an ambience, but also reminds us that details need to stay relevant at every level of our designs. Our project portfolio has a tremendous range in terms of type and scale: from restaurants and bars, clubs and hotels, and religious institutions to families looking to build a home or for somewhere to escape to for a holiday—even wildly theatrical one-night events. For me, the very first step of any project is always taking time to think about the narrative, as it sets the scene for all later design decisions.

Previous page, left: Private residence, Istanbul, Türkiye, 2003. Leather canvas and metal-mesh tent suspended in a wood-clad atrium over a divan to create a unique entrance.

Previous page, top right: Khaleeji restaurant, Cultural Village, Katara, Doha, Qatar, 2017. Modernized *majlis* (sitting room) seating with *mashrabiya* latticework paneling.

Previous page, bottom right: Private *yalı*, Istanbul, 2014. Traditional *sedir* seating in a pavilion next to a *yalı*.

Opposite, above: Private villa, Muscat, Oman, 2023. Design rendering for an entrance hall.

Opposite, below: Istanbul waterfront architecture inspires a concept study of a multipurpose culture and entertainment center in Karaköy, Istanbul, Türkiye, 2015.

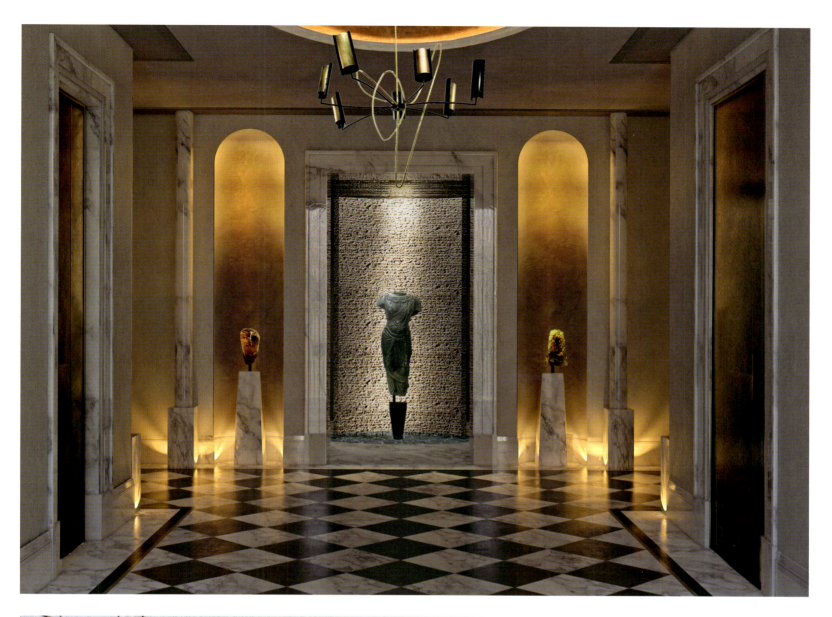

Masterpiece VIP Dining Room
(all images):

Top left: Jean Dubuffet, *Site avec 5 personnages*, 1981, acrylic on paper laid down on canvas, 50 x 67 cm, Bastian Gallery, above Peter Coker, *Aldeburgh I*, 1964, oil on panel, 121.9 x 121.9 cm, Jonathan Clark Fine Art, facing Michelangelo Cerquozzi, *Allegory of Autumn*, 1600s, oil on canvas, 73.5 x 144 cm, Robilant + Voena (*right*)—all located between tone-on-tone beige Iznik çini semi-arch with celadon-and-burgundy pendants, collaboration between Gorbon and Zeynep Fadıllıoğlu Design. Dados hand-painted in a gradient of silver-celadon-burgundy by Gordon Levine.

Top middle: Eighteenth-century mirror from James Graham-Stewart.

Top right : George Brookshaw fireplace from Butchoff Antiques, Selene Mirror from 88 Gallery, and Auguste Jean-Baptiste Vinchon, *Castle on the Shore, Early Morning*, c.1816, oil on canvas, 18.2 x 18.7 cm, Dickinson Gallery.

Bottom left: Evie from de Gournay's London design team.

Bottom middle: Murano mirror above eighteenth-century Franconian-style console, both from Rose Uniacke, placed between fabric columns and mini sofas upholstered with Zeynep's antique fabrics. Dados hand-painted in a gradient of silver-celadon-burgundy by Gordon Levine.

Bottom right: White peacock featured on de Gournay *Topkapı* hand-painted wallpaper, created in collaboration with Zeynep Fadıllıoğlu Design.

Left: Private mansion in Doha, Qatar, 2019. Design rendering for a living room.

Next pages: Six Senses Kocataş Mansions, Istanbul, Türkiye, 2019. Sketch for a reception room based on a typical *yalı* study.

I don't think of the design process as trying to create a perfect picture; it is quite intuitive, much like scenography, where we try to bring together all of the elements that will establish a certain atmosphere and spirit. Our mood boards are where the design language starts to develop; we look at a wide range of sources for inspiration—from art, objects, and books to photography and films—in order to establish a visual library.

I find personal inspiration in many places. Reading is very important to me, as well as watching films and documentaries. I particularly enjoy being around people who are not like me, otherwise creative discussions become a bit like talking to myself. This is why I always work with a team made up of very different personalities and expertise. You can't stay in your comfort zone. You must look around, travel, and surround yourself with difference so that you are constantly exposed to contrasting ideas.

When I work in a different culture, I like to spend time there, assess it, and view it from various perspectives. How a young person sees Paris or London is dramatically different from an older person, for example. It's very important for a designer to try to understand people so that they can narrate how someone lives now, and imagine how that may change in the future.

We have designed many restaurants and clubs, and I am convinced that part of our success in this field is because these interiors need a distinctive character and a coherent storyline that make the space memorable. I've always observed people in social situations, and noticed quite early on that setting the scene, right from the initial approach, is vital. The experience of a space starts before one enters, so rather than just designing a room we begin the process by thinking about who will arrive there, and how.

Previous pages: Six Senses Kocataş
Mansions, Istanbul, Türkiye, 2019.
Design rendering for a reception
room based on a typical *yalı* study.

Opposite: Çubuklu 29 Restaurant
Club and beach, 1987. Illustration of a
hand-painted Ottoman-inspired tent
with leather detailing by Kadir Akorak.

Above: Bird's-eye view of the
Çubuklu 29 complex. Aerial photo
taken by legendary aerobatic pilot
Murat Öztürk.

At the Çubuklu 29 Restaurant Club (1987), visitors arrive on the Asian
side of the Bosphorus after a five-minute ride in a simple wooden *taka*
(boat) from the European side of Istanbul. Our design narrative of
journeying to a lush, bucolic garden with pavilions and hand-painted
tents was not conceived for simply aesthetic purposes; it was practical
too. Although the site was idyllic, and the quay approach particularly
glamorous, we had just one month to design and build an outdoor
restaurant and bar on a 200-square-meter waterside plot, where we
were not permitted to build any permanent structures. I liked the idea
of creating a verdant retreat, but the restaurant and bar also had to
function efficiently. So, limited to just fifty square meters in which to
build a kitchen, we designed a traditional Ottoman kiosk with ten sides
that extended outward, allowing for maximum effectiveness. People
were astounded when they saw the previously barren parcel of land
transformed into a dramatic new landscape.

Once we have established the general mood for a project, I start to
visualize the entire experience as if I were inside the finished spaces, so
that I know how it would feel to be there. I explore like the frames of a
film, from different perspectives, and imagine the personality of someone
who might go there and what they would find enticing or surprising. This
is also important when it comes to planning the tactility of a space, since
the feel of furnishings—the plushness of a cushion or sofa, or the heft of a
hand-hammered bronze door handle—is very important to me.

Previous pages: The Peninsula Istanbul, Türkiye, 2023. Various crafted materials including (*clockwise from left*), liquid metal on stainless steel in satin-brass finish, inlaid mother-of-pearl, CNC-cut marble, and fused glass.

Opposite: The Peninsula Istanbul, Türkiye 2023. Restored staircase with original details set against a recent building addition that was clad in mirror to minimize its impact.

Tastes and styles change over time, especially with restaurants and bars, and if you don't have a strong narrative, they date very quickly. At the Nişantaşi Beymen Brasserie, Istanbul (2003), we paid tribute to classic French brasseries by creating the timeless, lively, and friendly ambience of a neighborhood café. The interior felt as if it had evolved over many years, with an abstract, patterned marble floor, and the juxtaposition of a Murano chandelier with metal-and-glass geometric lighting fixtures. We clad columns with dark lacquer, which helped to create a cozy atmosphere, and large mirrors helped to connect this to the outdoor terrace, where we placed classic French café-style wicker chairs. This all gave the Nişantaşi Beymen Brasserie narrative a coherence and authenticity.

We work on a great number of heritage projects, which means we often inherit a powerful story. For instance, at The Peninsula Istanbul (2023), we worked on four separate buildings—three of which are protected historical landmarks dating from the early 1900s. Each has been meticulously renovated in collaboration with the Heritage Board to ensure the design is in keeping with local history and culture, linking past and present to create an emotional connection between the architecture and the Bosphorus Strait—a convergence point of East and West.

Guests at a luxury heritage hotel expect depth of experience, although this can be expressed in a subtle way. In the spa, in the ceiling above the 25-meter swimming pool, *muqarnas*, traditional three-dimensional ornamentation, soften the lighting, transforming the perspective. We also paid attention to design elements like graphics, for instance the sculptural brass signage, and furnishings, such as the chairs in guest rooms that have an elegant Ottoman turban-inspired carved detail on the armrests. Throughout, details needed to be cogent, consistent, and unifying, while taking cues from the city's heritage.

Above: The Peninsula Istanbul Spa, Türkiye, 2023. Tepidarium, clad with Marmara marble and centered with a traditional fountain fixture.

Opposite: Thermal suites at the Spa of The Peninsula Istanbul, Türkiye, 2023. Curvilinear walls and ceiling clad in lapis lazuli Sicis glass mosaic; floor clad in beige Sicis Glimmer glass mosaic.

Next page, left: The Peninsula Istanbul, Türkiye, 2023. Lobby balustrade on the mezzanine floor, for which the original pattern was reproduced. Stainless-steel elements finished in satin brass and dark bronze.

Next page, right: The Peninsula Istanbul, Türkiye, 2023. Bauhaus-inspired, multilayered engraved glass with painted panels. A collaboration between Zeynep Fadıllıoğlu Design and glass artist Kerim Kılıçarslan.

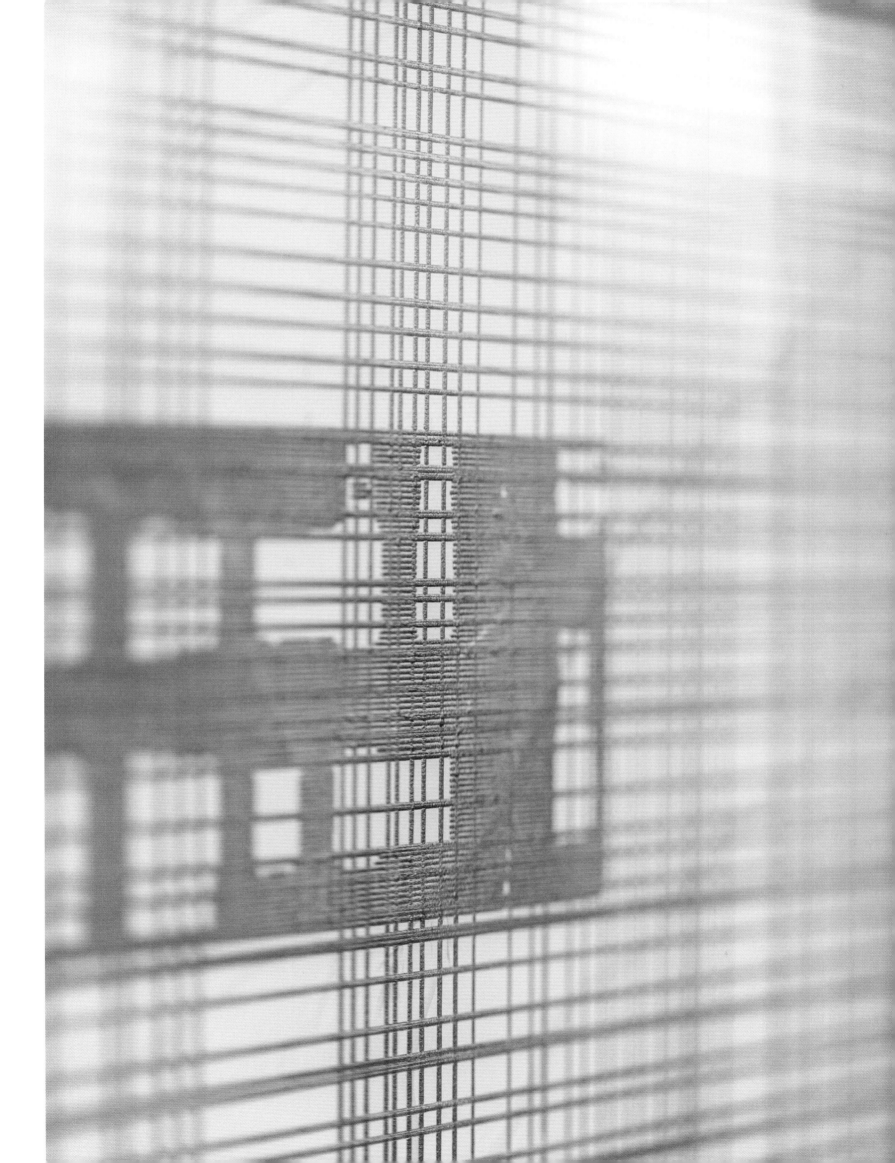

We recently proposed a powerful narrative for a five-star hotel project in Rome, Italy, that paid homage to the rich heritage of the Orient Express. We not only showed the glamor of travel by train but also took inspiration from each stop along the iconic train's journey from Paris to Constantinople during different eras, creating an exuberant storyline for different spaces in the hotel. Each interior reflected the character of a city along the route: the speakeasy evoked late eighteenth-century Istanbul, while the cigar lounge was reminiscent of 1970s Milan. Throughout, Italian art and design pieces created a link between the context and narrative. Some details were quite subtle and designed to be noticed over time, as I thought it was important that the story unfold gradually and artfully.

Above: Heritage hotel, Rome, Italy, 2021. Sketch for a rooftop terrace restaurant.

Opposite: Heritage hotel, Rome, Italy, 2021. Sketch for a teppanyaki restaurant.

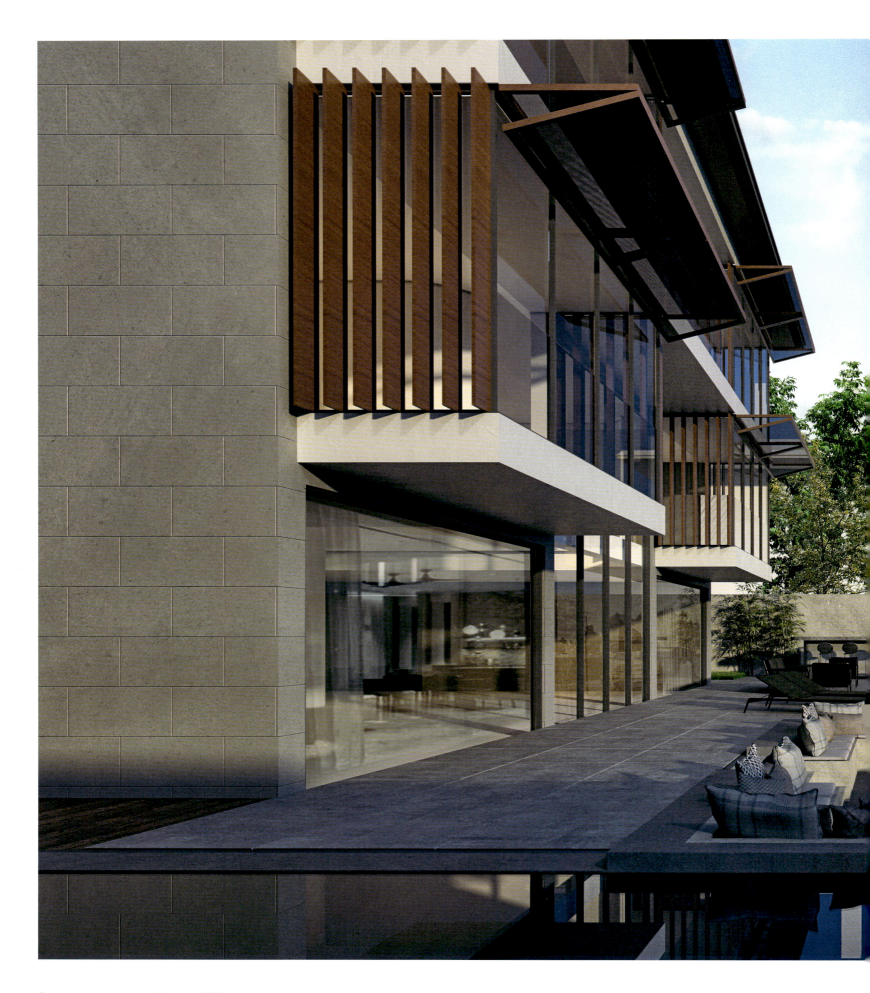

Private *yalı*, Istanbul, Türkiye, 2021.
Design rendering of a modernized
Bosphorus *yalı* with a foldable mesh
facade, sunken firepit, and pool.

The way we think about home design has changed dramatically over the decades. My mother's generation looked to other cultures—the French, Italian, and English—for the epitome of stylish living at home. Without even knowing it, people also tend to repeat what they have seen in films or houses abroad. I believe that designing a home is not about the scenery or creating a stage, but about layering memories and treasured artifacts to create a personal narrative.

There are always some projects that bring incredible joy, places that feed your soul. Inevitably for me, these are the ones where the design is not obvious. In India in 2005, we were asked to build three houses on one site, to be lived in by different generations of the same family. We wanted to devise quite a fluid experience focused on telling the family's story. A narrative helped me come up with a practical framework for the project that also needed to combine a range of tastes to suit each generation, from creative contemporary to glamorous and sophisticated. Our design proposal included a glass ceiling that connected all three houses, creating courtyards, expanding spaces visually, and blurring the boundaries between indoors and out. In a thoughtful narrative, space is just as important as physical constructs.

Above: Private beach villa, Muscat, Oman, 2023. Early concept sketch.

Opposite: Private residence, Istanbul, Türkiye, 2020. Digital rendering of the library design completed with Cassina armchairs by Afra and Tobia Scarpa.

Next page: Private villa in Muscat, Oman, 2023. A 3D computer rendering of a design to incorporate the client's art collection.

Recently, we designed the interiors of a home for a client in Oman who has a vast and eclectic collection of art and design, including exquisite jewelry and perfume bottles, sculptures, and antiques. Since there were so many pieces, and the family wanted to live with them all, we analyzed how they used each room, and how it felt to walk from one to the next, so that the narrative developed around circulation, bringing their collection into the routine of their daily life. We devised an elegant display system of translucent walls and niches so that the distinctive personal choices would emerge organically; the story continues outdoors with a contemporary sculpture drawing the eye toward the surrounding landscape.

Private villa in Muscat, Oman, 2023.
Design rendering for a dressing room.

Above: Ottoman bedroom at the *Daily Telegraph*/House & Garden Fair, London, UK, 2002. Gypsum medallion handmade by Kemal Cimbiz, molding cast after Çırağan Palace ornaments.

Right: Ottoman bedroom at the *Daily Telegraph*/House & Garden Fair, London, UK, 2002. Patinated walls by Gordon Levine.

Opposite, above: Four artworks framed as one: Canan Tolon, *Untitled*, 1999, rust and Rhoplex on canvas. Antique halberd (*teber*) used as artwork. Private residence, Istanbul, Türkiye, 2005. (Andrew Martin Interior Designer of the Year Award 2005)

Opposite, below: Private residence in Istanbul, Türkiye, 2005. Armor showcased in a stairwell on a specially molded Perspex frame.

Next page, left: Mosque, Astana, Kazakhstan, 2019. Design concept for a Central Asian mosque. Includes a 50-meter-high *mihrab* and a prayer area for 30,000 people.

Next page, right: Mosque, Stuttgart, Germany, 2018. Design concept for a European mosque. Interlocking arched buttresses and Seljuk architectural references in the *minbar* design.

Page 266: Mosque, Astana, Kazakhstan, 2019. Design concept for a Central Asian mosque. A 68,000-square-meter project with an 83-meter-high main dome.

Sometimes, when we are working with a real estate developer, we simply imagine who might live there, because without a story a space feels empty and has no soul. In 2009 in Istanbul, we were commissioned to design a show house that the viewer would feel they could move into immediately. One of the first things I did was to adjust the layout to add a sense of arrival and a more natural progression of moving through the home. Narrative helped me think about how to give movement a physical form and plan how spaces were revealed, flowed, and led into each other. Sequence is important; I added areas that would give a sense of what came next, or a pause before discovery. The design was so successful that the developer changed the layout of all the houses in the project.

One of my proudest moments was being selected to create an installation for the prestigious *Daily Telegraph*/House & Garden Fair at London's Olympia in 2002. I designed an Ottoman bedroom that showed a very modern way of living with heritage pieces. At the time, people suggested I avoid creating an enclosed immersive experience, but I felt strongly that this would be a powerful storyline and provide a new perspective. Then, in 2005, my design for the waterside Ulus Residence in Istanbul, which combines the traditional and avant-garde with a respect for place, convention, and other cultures, won the Modern Residential Interior category of the Design and Decoration Awards in London. That reconfirmed the importance of narrative for me, not as an end in itself but as a way of finding new relationships between the present and the past.

Even with religious buildings such as mosques, where each space already has a purpose and meaning, and their sequence is largely set, taking the time to develop a narrative helps reaffirm beliefs and traditions, and adds meaning and a sense of discovery to the unfolding spaces. This is why we have been able to combine tradition and modernity, bridging the old and the new. You must be in tune with your project, and the purpose for which it is being built, and only then does the narrative emerge.

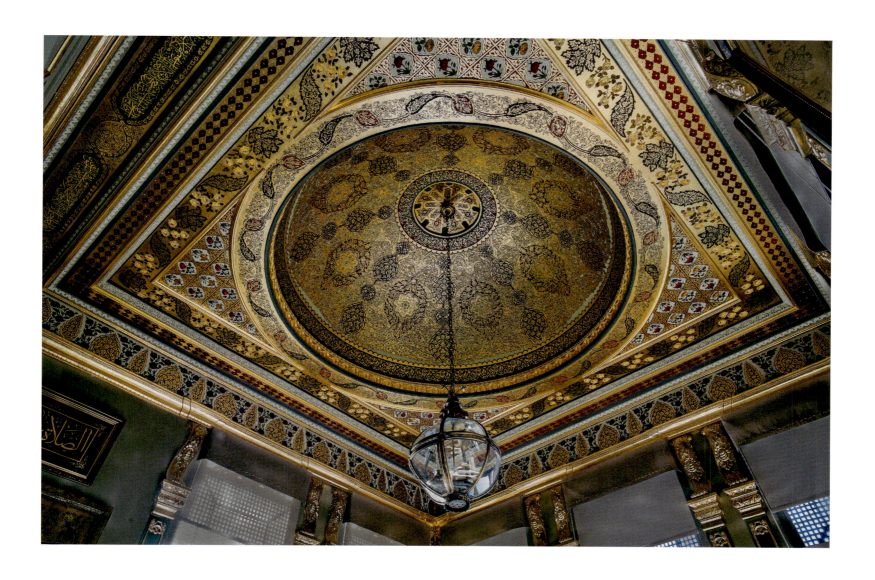

Opposite: Design concept for a mosque in Astana, Kazakhstan, 2019. Arcade featuring a vaulted ceiling with *kalemişi* faux-leather decoration.

Above: Private *yalı*, Istanbul, Türkiye, 2014. Restored *kalemişi* pencilwork on the antique dome ceiling.

Next page: Doha, Qatar, 2016. Rendering of an outdoor mosque design concept with a semi-transparent Moorish-patterned architectural envelope.

Left: The Spa, The Peninsula Istanbul, Türkiye, 2023. *Muqarnas*-bordered, cascaded dome with a metallic stucco finish.

Once we have established the general mood for a project, I start to visualize the entire experience as if I were inside the finished spaces, so that I know how it would feel to be there. I explore like the frames of a film, from different perspectives, and imagine the personality of someone who might go there and what they would find enticing or surprising.

Timeline of Selected Projects

Çubuklu 29
Restaurant Club
Istanbul, Türkiye
⌂ ⅋ ☼

• Vaniköy 29
Restaurant Club
Istanbul, Türkiye
⌂ ⅋ ☼

• Antalya 29
Restaurant Club
Antalya, Türkiye
⌂ ⅋ ☼

• Taxim Nightpark
Nightclub by Nigel
Coates & Doug Branson
Istanbul, Türkiye
〰

• Ulus 29 Restaurant Club
Istanbul, Türkiye
⅋ ☼

• Zeynep's home
Istanbul, Türkiye
⅋ ☼

| 1985 | 1987 | 1990 | 1993 | 1994 |

KEY

⌂ Architectural Design ▣ Concept Design ⓪ Design & Installation ⅋ Fit-out Construction

☼ Interior Design 〰 Design Management ⌒⌒ Facade ✳ Event ⅄ Award ⚘ Speaker

Andrew Martin
International Designer
of the Year Award 2002
♈

• Private residence
Istanbul, Türkiye
℘ ☼

Daily Telegraph/House
and Garden Fair
London, England
⊚

Bilgi University Design
Culture & Management
Chair (until 2012)
Istanbul, Türkiye
℗

• Keyf-han Restaurant
by Nigel Coates &
Doug Branson
Istanbul, Türkiye
⏜

• Event design at
Çırağan Palace
Istanbul, Türkiye
⚙

• Private residence
Hampstead
London, England
℘ ☼

• Chintamani Restaurant
London, England
℘ ☼

| 1996 | 1997 | 1998 | 2001 | 2002 |

Private residence
New Delhi, India
⚡

Modern Designer
of the Year Award
London, England
⚱

Private mansion
Baku, Azerbaijan
⚡

Sinbin Restaurant
Istanbul, Türkiye
♒ ⚡

Private residence
Istanbul, Türkiye
♒ ⚡

Hammam Shop
Istanbul, Türkiye
⚡

Private residence
Istanbul, Türkiye
♒ ⚡

Ulus residence
Istanbul, Türkiye
♒ ⚡

Private mansion
Bosphorus
Istanbul, Türkiye
♒ ⚡

Mardan Palace Hotel
Antalya, Türkiye
♒ ⚡

Private residence
Arnavutköy
Istanbul, Türkiye
♒ ⚡

Private residence
Istanbul, Türkiye
♒ ⚡

• Nişantaşı Beymen
Brasserie
Istanbul, Türkiye
♒ ⚡

• Farmhouse
New Delhi, India
⌂

• Hotel Les Ottomans
Bosphorus
Istanbul, Türkiye
♒ ⚡

• Event-South Göcek Bay
Muğla, Türkiye
✤

• Company headquarters
Istanbul, Türkiye
♒ ⚡

2003	2005	2006	2007	2008

KEY

⌂ Architectural Design   ◎ Concept Design   ⓪ Design & Installation   ♒ Fit-out Construction

⚡ Interior Design   ⌣ Design Management   ⌒⌒ Facade   ✤ Event   ⚱ Award   ⚲ Speaker

Sukar Pasha
Ottoman Lounge
Doha, Qatar
ૠ ☼

Private villa
Istanbul, Türkiye
ૠ ☼

Restaurant Qatar
Doha, Qatar
ૠ ☼

Stepevi Shop
New York, US
ૠ ☼

The WIFTS Foundation
International Visionary
Awards
Ψ

Private villa, Bosphorus
Istanbul, Türkiye
ૠ ☼

Club Ali Bey Resort
Antalya, Türkiye
☼

Private mansion
New Delhi, India
ૠ ☼

Private mansion
London, England
ૠ ☼

Estate developer—
Show house
Istanbul, Türkiye
ૠ ☼

Private villa
Vroondaal, Netherlands
ﬁﬁ ☼

• Kuum 29 Beach Club
Restaurant
Bodrum, Türkiye
ૠ ☼

Walk-in 29 Restaurant
Istanbul, Türkiye
ૠ ☼

• Private mansion
Muscat, Oman
ૠ ☼

• Şakirin Mosque
Istanbul, Türkiye
ﬁﬁ ૠ ☼

• Friday Mosque
Doha, Qatar
ૠ ☼

Golden Mosque
Doha, Qatar
ﬁﬁ ૠ ☼

Private mansion
Jeddah, Saudi Arabia
☼

Private mansion
Amman, Jordan
ૠ ☼

Burj Khalifa Mosque
Mihrab
Dubai, UAE
⦿

Aga Khan Award
Nomination for
Şakirin Mosque
Ψ

Four Seasons Bosphorus
wedding reception
Istanbul, Türkiye
❈

• Martı Hotel Taksim
Istanbul, Türkiye
ૠ ☼

Collection launch
Paris, France
⦿

| 2009 | 2010 | 2011 | 2012 | 2013 |

Multi-purpose culture
and entertainment
center
Istanbul, Türkiye
⊙

Bali hotel
Bali, Indonesia
⊙

Private mansion, Tarabya
Istanbul, Türkiye
 වේ ☼

Private residence
Bodrum, Türkiye
 වේ ☼

Zeynep Fadıllıoğlu
Design Studio
Istanbul, Türkiye
 වේ ☼

Private villa, Bodrum
Bodrum, Türkiye
වේ ☼

Molu Fine Jewelry Shop
Istanbul, Türkiye
 වේ ☼

Maldives
Hospitality Project
Maldives
⊙

Fenix Istanbul
Restaurant
Istanbul, Türkiye
 වේ ☼

• Private *yalı*
Istanbul, Türkiye
 වේ ☼

Private residence
Istanbul, Türkiye
 වේ ☼

Zeynep's home
London, England
 වේ ☼

• Rooftop restaurant
Doha, Qatar
 වේ ☼

Restaurant Doha
Doha, Qatar
 වේ ☼

Mosque
Doha, Qatar
⊙

Jewelry design
for Atasay
Istanbul, Türkiye
⊙

Glass design
Istanbul, Türkiye
⊙

Company headquarters
Istanbul, Türkiye
 වේ ☼

• Beach tents
Doha, Qatar
 වේ ☼

Qatar boutique hotel
Doha, Qatar
⊙

Khaleeji restaurant
Doha, Qatar
⊙

Concrete tent
Doha, Qatar
 වේ ☼

Mosque Riyadh 1
Riyadh, Saudi Arabia
⊙

Mosque Riyadh 2
Riyadh, Saudi Arabia
⊙

Private residence
Istanbul, Türkiye
 වේ ☼

Private residence
Istanbul, Türkiye
 වේ ☼

• Princes' Islands Boutique
Hotel Club House
Istanbul, Türkiye
 වේ ☼

Fenix Restaurant Club
Bodrum, Türkiye
 වේ ☼

Club Anjelique
Bodrum, Türkiye
 වේ ☼

Mosque
Stuttgart, Germany
⊙

• Ulus 29 Restaurant
Club Redesign
Istanbul, Türkiye
☼ ⌣

Nahita Restaurant
(now named Nusr-Et)
Boston, US
☼ ⌣

Friday Mosque
Manama, Bahrain
☼

LET'S TALK –Nata
Supernova
Antalya, Türkiye
⬜

| 2014 | 2015 | 2016 | 2017 | 2018 |

KEY

⌂ Architectural Design ⊙ Concept Design ⦿ Design & Installation වේ Fit-out Construction

☼ Interior Design ⌣ Design Management ⌒⌒ Facade ⊞ Event ⬚ Award ⬜ Speaker

Central Asia mosque
Astana, Kazakhstan
⬡

• Six Senses Kocataş
Mansions
Istanbul, Türkiye
⬡

Private mansion
Doha, Qatar
☼

Design Week Turkiye
Istanbul, Türkiye
⬡

Design Shanghai -
Andrew Martin
Shanghai, China
⬡

Cultural complex
Doha, Qatar
⬡

Private residence
Istanbul, Türkiye
⬡

• Meeting hall
Doha, Qatar
꠲ ☼

Private residence
Istanbul, Türkiye
⬡

Private yalı
Istanbul, Türkiye
☼

• Private beach house
Kuwait City, Kuwait
☼

Heritage hotel
Rome, Italy
⬡

Masterpiece Art Fair
London, England
⬿

• Royal tomb
Amman, Jordan
⬿

Private villa
Muscat, Oman
꠲ ☼

Private beach villa
Muscat, Oman
☼

• The Peninsula Istanbul
Istanbul, Türkiye
☼ ꠵

The Pearl Mosque
Doha, Qatar
꠲ ☼

| 2019 | 2020 | 2021 | 2022 | 2023 |

Biographies and Acknowledgments

Zeynep Fadıllıoğlu

Born in 1955 in Istanbul, Türkiye, Zeynep grew up in a waterside *yalı* in Yeniköy on the European shore of the Bosphorus. After studying Computer Science in England at the University of Sussex, she went on to train in Art History and Design at the Inchbald School of Design, in London.

Zeynep's career began with the design and creation of more than twenty restaurant and club interiors for her husband, Metin Fadıllıoğlu, who is widely credited with creating the modern artistic dining scene in Istanbul.

In 1995 she opened the Zeynep Fadıllıoğlu Design and Architecture Office. Zeynep has since designed and project-managed the construction of prestigious private residences and yachts, hotels, restaurants and clubs, company headquarters, and luxury-goods shops in Azerbaijan, Bahrain, France, Germany, India, Jordan, Kuwait, the Maldives, Oman, Qatar, Saudi Arabia, Türkiye, the United Kingdom, and the United States. She is believed to be the first woman ever to design a mosque, the Şakirin Mosque in Istanbul, which has become a symbol of unity, and was nominated for the Aga Khan Award for Architecture in 2010.

For fourteen years, Zeynep lectured on Design Management and Culture at Istanbul Bilgi University. She is featured annually in one of the industry's foremost publications, *The Andrew Martin Design Review*, and won their International Designer of the Year Award in 2002. The same year she was also one of only four designers asked to design a bedroom for the *Daily Telegraph*/House & Garden Fair. This was said to be one of the most visited parts of the fair. In 2005 Zeynep won Modern Designer of the Year at the London Design and Decoration awards, and in 2010 she received the Women's International Film and Television Showcase (WIFTS) International Visionary Award.

In 2012, Zeynep launched the Zeynep Fadıllıoğlu Product Line; in 2013, the Zeynep Fadıllıoğlu Design Furniture Collection premiered at the Paris Maison&Objet fair. The contemporary pieces, designed to suit modern lifestyles, draw on Türkiye's rich culture and history—its Anatolian, Byzantine, Seljuk, and Ottoman roots—and highlight traditional handcrafting techniques.

Zeynep's recent projects include the interiors concept for Six Senses Kocataş Mansions, a group of renovated Ottoman-era buildings at the edge of the Bosphorus (2019); a private beach house in Kuwait (2021); two private mansions in Muscat (2023); and The Pearl Mosque (2023), a 5,100-square-meter landmark monument in Doha, Qatar. She was also responsible for the interiors of The Peninsula Istanbul, a renovated 177-bedroom, four-building heritage property on the banks of the Bosphorus (2023).

Zeynep has offices in Istanbul, London, Muscat, and Doha.

Acknowledgments

There are so many people who have helped to make this book, and whose support over the years has been invaluable to the projects we have highlighted in these pages.

I have been fortunate to work with wonderful clients and patrons, and, as every designer knows, their confidence and support is key to any project. At the same time, there have been many others who have also played an important role in my design journey. They include Nejma Beard, Yüksel Behlil, Anne Becker Olins, Sue Crewe, Clive Crook, Jacqueline Duncan, Michael Inchbald, Viscount Linley, Oğuz Özerdem, Atul Punj, Fritz von der Schulenburg, Lord John Scott, Ghazi and Ghada Shaker, Çiğdem Simavi, Sarah Stewart-Smith, and Martin Waller.

I would also like to acknowledge the exceptional artists and master craftspeople, *usta*, with whom I have worked to transform ideas into reality: Işık Akbaygil, Kadir Akorak, Marc Brazier-Jones, Abdurrahman Bülbül, Nahide Büyükkaymakçı, Marie-Severine de Caraman Chimay, Ermano Casasco, Jemma Cave, Arnold Chan, Steve Charles, Kemal Cımbız, Tuncay Dem, Ahmet Ertuğ, Fiona Flint, Aziz and Orhan Gorbon, Hannah Cecil Gurney, Sevan Hafidu, Mahmut Kahraman, Kaya Kalaycı, Ömer Karasu, Kerim Kılıçarslan, Orhan Koçan, Ahmet Kolçak, Gordon Levine, Lilou Marquand, Léopold Marraud des Grottes, Antuan Nurhan, Doğan Paksoy, Alev Sağlam, Recep Ali Serbest, Abdurrahman Sevil, Lisa Shamash, Sally Storey, Tarun Tahillani, Fatih Tekden, Hasan Ulutaş, and Alaaddin Usta.

I am also most grateful to the writers and editors who have supported my work: Michael Adams, Fatih Altaylı, Nina Azzarello, Dominic Bradbury, Ed Cumming, Anne McElvoy, Çağdaş Ertuna, Andrew Finkel, Antoine Galimard, Tony Gallagher, Jaqui Gifford, Michael Hodges, Roula Khalaf, Birgit Lohmann, Valeri Mallet de Givry, J.S. Marcus, Sheenaa McKenzie, Scott Mini, Zafer-Nüket Mutlu, Ertuğrul Özkök, Guillaume Perrier, Adrian Pielou, Carla Power, Nick Redman, Rin Simson, and Sarah Stewart-Smith.

I would also like to thank my team at Zeynep Fadıllıoğlu Design: Kayıhan Akipek, Burçin Akyazı, Merve Alagöz, Ece Alkan, Ebru Aslan, Meltem Ateş Kaygusuz, Burçin Balcı Çınar, Can Başak, Atakan Baydar, Yüksel Behlil, Serra Çizmeci, Nalan Çorlu Bilginer, Serpil Demircioğlu, Çağatay Efe, Didem Eroğul, Ehsan Ensafi, Levent Furgaç, Buğra Güler, Selmin Hamulu Yeşilyurt, Eray İznik, Beste Koç, Esra Kurt, Simla Köksal, Tuna Kuru, Meltem Özgür, Selin Tara, Cansu Tarı Dağ, Gülay Terzi Yukarıgöz, Samet Toprakçı, and Hasan Yılmaz. I am particularly grateful to Özlem Akçor, İdil Erdemli, and Hülya Yıldırım, who have been invaluable in helping to present the story of our work.

My thanks to the author, Catherine Shaw, who has been a maestra in conducting this book as a harmonious symphony from start to finish, and I am most grateful to the expert Rizzoli team of Alexia Casaús Leppo, Cecilia Curti, and Sara Saettone, led by Francesco Baragiola Mordini, and the editorial team of Akkadia Press, Jenny Bateman-Irish, designer Iain Hector, and proofreader Ian McDonald, led by Anne Renahan.

I would like to express my special thanks to Sir Michael Kadoorie for writing the foreword, and to his team of Peter Borer, Jason Daniels, Alistair Gough, Clement Kwok, Christobel Liao, and John Miller at The Peninsula Istanbul.

Above all, my deepest thanks to my beloved husband Metin, whose steadfast support, both professional and personal, is my bedrock, and to the greatest inspiration for the future of Zeynep Fadıllıoğlu Design, my grandchildren, Sinan, Defne, and Aylin Tara.

Previous page: Zeynep and Metin Fadillioglu, The Peninsula Istanbul, Türkiye (2023).

Catherine Shaw

Catherine Shaw is a writer, editor, and consultant, specializing in architecture and design. Originally an urban and environmental planner, she has lived in Hong Kong and Japan for thirty years.

Catherine wrote the *Wallpaper* Tokyo City Guide* and currently writes the *Louis Vuitton City Guide Hong Kong*. She edited *The Philosophy of Design* (Yanagi Design Studio, 2015), the first English translation of Japanese product designer Sori Yanagi's design essays, and is the author of *Hong Kong: Heritage, Art and Dreams* (Assouline, 2018) and *André Fu: Crossing Cultures with Design* (Thames & Hudson, 2020).

Since 2022, Catherine has written books for Rizzoli about Hong Kong–based art collector and designer Alan Chan; on the design philosophy of architect, artist, and collector William Lim; and produced a monograph on Beijing-based OPEN Architecture's cultural projects across China. She also contributed to a book on Hong Kong jewelry brand Qeelin, published by Assouline (2022).

Catherine advises architecture and design studios on key trends, and is a regular speaker and moderator at design events. She is the Asia-Pacific contributing editor for the magazine *Metropolis*, and is currently writing a book on Japanese architecture and another on The Peninsula London.

Acknowledgments

It takes many people to create a book, starting in this case with Anne Becker Olins, whose kind introduction to Zeynep sparked a conversation between us that has opened my eyes to a new world of design. Living in Hong Kong meant that, until then, my focus had inevitably been on Asia, so I am most grateful to have discovered a fascinating new sphere of art, craft, and design.

It has been a great privilege to delve into Zeynep's life's work over the past year, and throughout she has been especially generous in sharing her thoughts and trusting me with writing her story. It feels right that this book should be told from her own perspective, and that the rich visuals should, in addition to stunning project photographs and hand-drawn illustrations, include some of the outstanding historic and contemporary inspirations that contribute to her unique approach.

None of this would have been possible without the patience and passion of Zeynep's dedicated team, to whom I am deeply indebted. They include Özlem Akçor, for her indefatigable spirit in managing every step creating this book; İdil Erdemli, for her advice on all things design; and Hülya Yıldırım, whose encyclopedic visual memory underpins the selection of unforgettable images presented in this book. My thanks also to Simla Köksal and Gülay Terzi. Appreciation too for Serpil Demircioğlu, who plied us with Turkish tea and snacks as we worked in the team's Istanbul office on the banks of the Bosphorus.

At the heart of everything, behind the scenes, is Zeynep's husband, Metin, whose unfailing support and expert opinion has been invaluable throughout.

I would also like to express my appreciation to Sir Michael Kadoorie, whose engaging foreword provides illuminating insights into Zeynep's work.

Special thanks go to my husband, Alistair Gough, and children, Alexandra and Francesca, for their unwavering love, support, and patience in all things. I am also grateful to Clare Wadsworth for her professional research, editorial support, and friendship.

I am beholden to Francesco Baragiola Mordini at Rizzoli for his patience and guidance, and to his team—Alexia Casaús Leppo, Cecilia Curti, and Sara Saettone—for their expert assistance. My special gratitude goes to the editorial team of Anne Renahan of Akkadia Press, particularly editor Jenny Bateman-Irish and designer Iain Hector, not only for expertly guiding the book process but for always being so sympathetic to new ideas and suggestions. Thanks are also due to Ian McDonald for his rigor in proofreading the texts.

Glossary

Anatolia
Anatolia, also called Asia Minor, is the Asian peninsula of Türkiye.

architrave
Decorative molding surrounding a doorway, arch, or window.

baluster
A vertical rod or post between the hand and base rails of a staircase.

Bauhaus
The Bauhaus movement was founded in 1919 in Weimar by German architect Walter Gropius (1883–1969) and became the most influential modernist art school of the twentieth century.

Bursa
A historically significant city in north-western Türkiye renowned for its woolen, silk, and velvet fabrics in the fifteenth and sixteenth centuries.

Byzantine Empire
The eastern half of the Roman Empire, which survived for a thousand years after the western half had crumbled into feudal kingdoms, and which fell to the Ottoman Turks in 1453.

çini
Traditional glazed tiles and other architectural ceramics made from clay containing quartz and lime that are hand made in Türkiye.

Fabergé
The House of Fabergé was founded in 1842 in St Petersburg, Russia, and is best-known for its decorative gem-encrusted enamel Easter eggs.

hammam
Traditional public bathhouse with steam rooms modeled on ancient Roman baths, often featuring domed ceilings, regal columns, and marble interiors.

ikat
A patterned fabric made using warp and/or weft threads that are tie-dyed before weaving.

Iznik ware
Sixteenth- and seventeenth-century Turkish decorative ceramics made in İznik in western Anatolia.

kalemişi
Traditional hand-painted ornamental decoration.

Khorasan-style plaster
Traditional brick-lime plaster mortar with waterproof properties typical of a province in northeastern Iran.

kilim
A rug made from interwoven rather than knotted wool, so that the surface is flat.

köşk
English: kiosk. Originally a small garden pavilion, open on some or all sides, common in the Ottoman Empire from the thirteenth century onward.

Marmara
A white marble with distinctive linear veins of gray, mined on Marmara Island, a district of Balıkesir, Türkiye.

mashrabiya
A highly decorative architectural element with carved wood latticework that serves as a window screen, allowing light and breezes to pass through the pattern.

mihrab
The niche in the wall of a mosque that indicates the direction of Mecca.

minbar
A short flight of steps in a mosque used as a pulpit by an imam.

muqarnas
Three-dimensional, scalloped geometric decoration common to Islamic architecture.

Murano
Venetian island renowned for blown-glass creations.

Ottoman Empire
Empire that controlled much of southeastern Europe, western Asia, and northern Africa between the fourteenth and early twentieth centuries.

pendeloque
A usually pear-shaped glass pendant used for ornamenting a lamp or chandelier.

saltillo
An unsealed terra-cotta tile originally from Saltillo, Coahuila, Mexico.

sedir
A modern interpretation of the traditional low, sprawling seating without a back or armrest, typical of Ottoman palaces.

Seljuk Empire
Medieval Turco-Persian, Sunni Muslim empire based in central Anatolia from 1050 to 1300 AD.

Steppes
Geographical term describing an area of treeless grassland plains.

sudare
Traditional Japanese screens or blinds made of wood, bamboo, or other natural materials.

taka
A traditional small boat built and used on the Black Sea shores of Türkiye.

Tophane ware
Pottery named after the area of Istanbul in which it was manufactured in the late nineteenth century. Distinctively orange-red but also black and paler brown, the decoration is either carved, molded, or stamped and frequently embellished with gilt.

yalı
Waterside residences built from the eighteenth to twentieth centuries along the Bosphorus, originally used as summerhouses.

Credits

Artwork

p. 76 © Alex Katz by SIAE 2023

p. 95 © Andre Putman by SIAE 2023

p. 77 © Anish Kapoor. All rights reserved, DACS/SIAE 2023

Back Cover, pp. 78–79, 83–84 © Ivan Navarro by SIAE 2023

pp. 72–73 © Jaume Plensa by SIAE 2023

p. 232 © Jean Dubuffet by SIAE 2023

p. 111 © Juian Opie by SIAE 2023

p. 104 © Komet by SIAE 2023

pp. 64, 96, 98–99 © Peter Beard by SIAE 2023

p. 87 © Ruud Van Empel by SIAE 2023

p. 80 © Thorsten Brinkmann by SIAE 2023

Photography

Ahmet Ertuğ endpapers, pp. 14–15

Belgin Çöleri p. 190

Ben Fisher pp. 232–233 (far left, bottom)

Berna Bal pp. 36, 71, 212, 240

Bige Yalın pp. 10, 191, 280

Bradley Secker cover and pp. 30, 34, 35, 37, 54–55, 56, 57, 66, 68, 88–89, 90–91, 98–99, 105, 106, 107, 121, 123, 124–125, 129, 130, 131, 132–133, 134, 141, 145, 150, 151, 158–159, 162, 174, 176, 177, 179, 180, 181, 182–183, 184, 186, 187, 188, 193, 201, 202–203, 207, 208, 209, 211, 214–215, 218, 219, 224, 242–243, 244, 246, 247, 248, 249, 272, 275 (fourth from left), 279 (fifth from left)

Brian Mckee pp. 72–73, 74–75, 76, 77, 78–79, 204, 229 (bottom), 269, 278 (far left), back cover

Cengiz Dikbaş p. 156

de GOURNAY pp. 220, 232–233 (top, far, second, and third from left; bottom third from left)

Ehsan Ensafi pp. 172

Emre Dörter p. 135 (top and bottom)

Enea Landscape Architecture p. 31

Engin Aydeniz pp. 112, 155

Erginoğlu & Çalışlar Architecture p. 276 (second from left)

Fevzi Ondu pp. 45, 80, 81, 87, 110

Fritz Von Der Schulenburg pp. 20, 70, 164, 165, 166, 274 (fifth from left), 275 (second from left), 276 (third from left), 277 (far left)

Hit-Photography.com pp. 18, 21, 22, 24–25, 26, 27, 38, 40, 95, 96–97, 118, 126–127, 137, 142, 146, 148, 149, 163, 189, 277 (second, third, fourth from left), 278 (second, third from left)

İstanbul Üniversitesi Nadir Eserler Kütüphanesi pp. 28–29, 41

John Athimaritis pp. 52–53, 144, 210, 279 (far left)

Koray Erkaya pp. 46, 64, 67, 92, 93, 152–153, 160–161, 206, 228, 262, 274 (far left, second from left, fourth from left), 275 (third from left)

Metin Fadıllıoğlu pp. 196–197, 274 (third from left)

Murat Öztürk p. 241

Reto Guntli and Agi Simoes pp. 48, 49, 50–51, 200, 217, 278 (fourth from left)

Sadberk Hanım Museum p. 178

Salt Research, Monograph Archive (Courtesy of IFEA) pp. 226–227

Serkan Eldeleklioğlu pp. 6–7, 58–59, 60, 83, 84–85, 86, 101, 102–103, 104, 111, 113, 114, 120, 128, 140, 154, 157, 167, 168, 192, 216, 278 (fifth from left)

SUNA-INAN KIRAÇ FOUNDATION / Pera Museum pp. 175, 194–195

The Peninsula Istanbul pp. 32–33

Tricia de Courcy Ling pp. 198–199, 275 (fifth from left)

Zeynep Fadıllıoğlu Design Team pp. 42–43, 108–109, 138–139, 213, 229 (top), 231, 232–233 (bottom second from left), 234–235, 236–237, 238–239, 250, 251, 252–253, 254, 255, 256–257, 258–259, 260, 261, 264, 265, 266–267, 268, 270, 271, 275 (far left), 276 (far left), 276 (fourth from left), 276 (fifth from left), 277 (fifth from left), 279 (second, third, fourth from left)

Distributed in English throughout the world
by Rizzoli International Publications Inc.
300 Park Avenue South
New York, NY 10010, United States

ISBN: 978-88-918383-2-2

2023 2024 2025 2026 / 10 9 8 7 6 5 4 3 2 1

First edition: March 2024

Özlem Akçor – Lead Project Coordinator
Hülya Yıldırım – Design Coordinator
İdil Erdemli – Editorial & Design Coordinator
Anne Renahan – Project Manager
Iain Hector – Graphic Designer
Jenny Bateman-Irish – Editorial Manager
Ian McDonald – Proofreader

Editorial Note

Some of the references in this book include Turkish names or places: where this is relevant, letters particular to the Turkish alphabet have been used: ç, ğ, ı, ö, ş, ü (capitals are used for proper nouns, regardless).

Disclaimer

The information contained in this publication, including all bibliographic and other references, was verified to the extent possible. The author and publisher cannot be held liable for any errors that arise after going to press.

This volume was printed at O.G.M. SpA
Via 1ª Strada, 87 – 35129 Padova

Visit us online:
Facebook.com/RizzoliNewYork
Twitter: @Rizzoli_Books
Instagram.com/RizzoliBooks
Pinterest.com/RizzoliBooks
Youtube.com/user/RizzoliNY
Issuu.com/Rizzoli

Front cover: The Peninsula Istanbul, Türkiye, 2023: *Muqarnas*-patterned domes align above the pool where the Marmara-clad columns are submerged in water, reminiscent of a cistern, a typical typology in ancient Istanbul. Coated tempered-steel artworks by Osman Dinç: *Untitled*, 2022.

Back cover: Nejad Devrim, *Soyut Kompozisyon (Abstract Composition)*, 1948 and 1950, two oil-on-canvas paintings above geometric marble consoles. Consoles, rock-crystal, and brass chandelier by Hervé Van der Straeten. Beneath the staircase, a hand-painted *kalemişi* mural, gilt architrave from Edirne and Iván Navarro, *Burden*, 2011, in blue neon, plexiglass, mirror, wood, paint. Private *yalı*, Istanbul, Türkiye, 2014.

Endpapers: Modernized *muqarnas* pattern created by combining the three-piece CNC-cut marble units by hand, photographed by renowned artist and photographer Ahmet Ertuğ, The Spa at the Peninsula Istanbul, Türkiye, 2023.

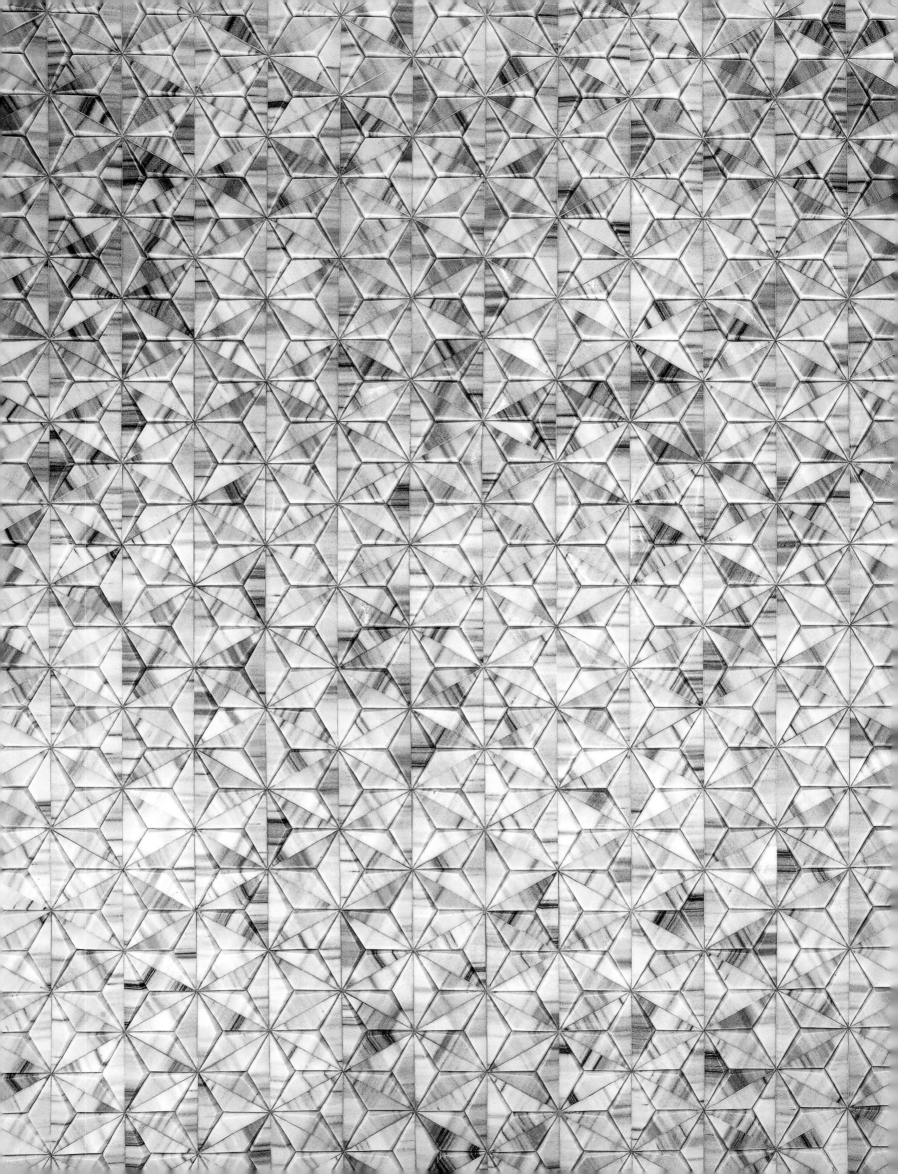